Fully Funded

The Christian Missionary's 7-Step Guide
to Raising Support and Growing Your
Donor Base in Today's Modern World

Mike Kim *and* Mary Valloni

Fully Funded

The Christian Missionary's 7-Step Guide
to Raising Support and Growing Your
Donor Base in Today's Modern World

Endorsements

"Mary Valloni and Mike Kim are invaluable resources, offering expertise and practical insights. Their book presents a clear, actionable plan that is easy to implement and yields noticeable results. As both a support raiser and a trainer in the field, I highly recommend *Fully Funded* for its exceptional guidance and effectiveness."

Delyn Cole
National Director of Coaching and Support Raising Training
Chi Alpha Campus Ministries, USA

"*Fully Funded* is the "secret decoder ring" that so many missionaries have been waiting for. I am a missionary and coach missionaries, and what Mike and Mary have curated and distilled here provides an approachable, insightful, strategic understanding of fundraising specific to the missionary community. But the "it" factor of this book is how Mike and Mary go beyond concepts and strategies and get right down to the tactical how-to part of fundraising. I could hand this book to a new missionary with no other training and simply advise, "Read this and do everything it says." That missionary would be fully funded."

James Harrington
CEO and Founder
Ugandan Water Project

"Mike and Mary have created a masterpiece for missionaries and nonprofit fundraisers. Their experience is vast, their credibility rich, and their results undeniable. As a communicator, I've often been haunted by Benjamin Franklin's words, 'Well done is better than well said.' To say something well is one thing; to implement a God-given vision with abundant provision is another. Mike and Mary will help you do both. If you apply the principles of *Fully Funded*, I believe you will see a thirty-, sixty-, or even hundredfold return on your current fundraising endeavors."

Joshua Finley
Author, Coach, Pastor
My Freedom Church, Bel Air, MD

"From the perspective of an executive director of a regional parachurch youth ministry, I can't recommend *Fully Funded* by Mike Kim and Mary Valloni enough. Thanks to their method, I've launched ten ministry sites and raised over $3.5 million. Their practical strategies and heartfelt encouragement were game-changers for me. Their guidance can transform your journey just like it did mine. I love their work, and I want everyone to experience the success that the *Fully Funded* method brings."

Adam Strunz
Executive Director
Northern Plains Youth For Christ

"I have a background in ministry, and now I'm an entrepreneur. We are able to do more good for the kingdom with money than without. I see *Fully Funded* by Mike and Mary as a critical resource. This book doesn't just teach practical fundraising techniques—it aligns readers with godly principles about money and enterprise that can truly impact the world for Christ. I urge others to embrace this book and understand how to fund their mission effectively and righteously."

Billy Sticker
Author, The Blessed Entrepreneur
Founder of ChiroCandy.com

"It's one thing to have a dream; it's another to have the finances to fulfill it. In *Fully Funded*, Mary and Mike pour out wisdom, strategy, and practical advice for ministry leaders to put feet to their prayers and reach the destination that burns in their hearts. With their help, from a small garage in the back-end of Brazil, I raised up a network of evangelists in 24 nations."

Giles Stevens
Evangelist and Founder
The Great Mission

"Read *Fully Funded* and learn to fundraise like a pro. This strategies in this book helped us stay on top of new trends and organize our fundraising in more effective ways. But most importantly, it gave us an entirely new perspective and approach that focuses on what God is doing and not on ourselves."

Rob and Nichole Plaster
Full-time faith-based workers serving 20+ years in Europe

"Having experienced the challenges of support-raising as a missionary overseas, with not a huge network, we can truly appreciate the impact of *Fully Funded* by Mike Kim and Mary Valloni. Their insightful strategies and genuine encouragement reshaped our approach and gave us the tools to achieve success. This book is indispensable. It transformed our path, and it has the power to do the same for you."

Liz and Uli Mannchen
Founders
Lionhood and Live As Lions

"Mary Valloni and Mike Kim changed my life when they taught me the material in this book! I can say yes to so many things God gives me to do since I'm fully funded now. The relief from strain and the freedom to focus on ministry instead of fundraising—it's priceless! I thank God for Mike and Mary every time I think of them."

Nora McNamara
SIL International Language and Culture Learning Coordinator

"As the leader of an organization that provides nonprofit covering, strategic counsel, and care for Christian leaders who raise support, I encourage anyone on a fundraising journey to pick up this book. This is a wonderfully practical resource. Although every part of the process is useful, the concept of enlisting a team is a vital and fruitful part of the support raising process that is often missed. Pick up *Fully Funded*, work through the chapters, and see how God shows up!"

Morgan Funke
CEO
The Cause

"This is it! This is the book, this is the framework. Finally, someone (Mary and Mike) demystifies this outdated process of support raising and gives us all a straightforward path to follow, step by step. We wandered around the support-raising desert in circles for years before we found this and then within 90 days we were fully funded! Seven years later, Mary is still my coach and advisor, walking me into even bolder asks and expansions of our ministry."

Christian and Hannah Swails
Founders
CoCreation

"As an independent missionary in South India, I was clueless about where to begin. This book will help you clarify your vision, connect better with your sponsors, and reach your financial goals. Regardless of your location, these steps will help you become fully funded. I highly recommend *Fully Funded!*"

Kristina Blesson
Blesson International Ministries, India

"As a missionary, I know firsthand how overwhelming support-raising can be. The concepts taught in *Fully Funded* by Mike Kim and Mary Valloni completely transformed my mindset. Their practical strategies and heartfelt encouragement provided me with the roadmap I needed to get results. If you're a missionary or church leader looking to fund your mission, this book is an absolute must-read. It changed my journey, and it can change yours too."

Renée Treeyanon
World Mission Continuum Missionary, Thailand

"I have needed to raise funds many times over for 30+ years of our campus missionary work. To borrow the old adage, "I wish I knew then what I know now", Mary Valloni and Mike Kim are God-sends who have reset my mindset, attitude, and approach to support-raising in the last five years of missions work, and set me up for success now as a nonprofit ministry entrepreneur. I have often told many others that I am a disciple of the Lord Jesus Christ, AND Mary and Mike. I have participated as a learner in their Fully Funded Academy and all its added-value webinars, podcasts, and resources. *Fully Funded* will help any missionary, ministry director, or nonprofit leader know the principles, strategies, and best practices to reach their fundraising goals in order to fulfill their mission."

Steve Bortner
Founder and Executive Director
Crossing Cultures Making Disciples

"Having served on eight non-profit boards over the years, I can say with confidence that *Fully Funded* is the guide every organization needs. This book goes beyond just fundraising; it's a roadmap to mission clarity, organizational health, and meaningful donor relationships. The steps outlined here will not only ensure that your organization meets its financial goals but also make the impact God's called to achieve. I'll be recommending *Fully Funded* to every non-profit I'm involved with—this is a must-read for any organization serious about fulfilling its mission."

Robert Fukui
President
i61, inc.

"I've trained 1000+ missionaries in support raising and this book blew me away. Mike and Mary say the quiet parts out loud. From developing marketing to working out the practicals, *Fully Funded* can guide a missionary through a process of success. Missions can be scary and support raising is the number one reason why many don't make it to the field. This book is the catalyst and difference-maker a new generation of pioneers need."

Alex Seidler
Founder & Director
The Gateway Project

"Most missionaries would rather do anything than raise financial support, often choosing to live below their budget. But *Fully Funded* by Mike Kim and Mary Valloni changes that. This book is a step-by-step guide to building strong, lasting partnerships and raising the support you need. It's like a GPS for your fundraising journey—helping you track progress, adjust plans, and stay on course. Personally, it took me from 60% to 120% of my budget in a year. If your support-raising feels stuck, this motivational and practical guide is exactly what you need!"

Dr. Don Allen
Mosaic Initiatives
DonAndKaren.com

Fully Funded

The Christian Missionary's 7-Step Guide to Raising Support and Growing Your Donor Base in Today's Modern World

Mike Kim *and* Mary Valloni

All Scripture quotations, unless otherwise indicated, are taken from the Holy Bible, New International Version®, NIV®. Copyright ©1973, 1978, 1984, 2011 by Biblica, Inc.™ Used by permission of Zondervan. All rights reserved worldwide. www.zondervan.com. The "NIV" and "New International Version" are trademarks registered in the United States Patent and Trademark Office by Biblica, Inc.™

Published by Mike Kim and Mary Valloni, FullyFundedAcademy.com

Cover and Interior design by Jason Clement - clementcreativegroup.com

Paperback: 9798218539269

Ebook: 9798218539269

Audiobook: 9798218539269

To contact the authors directly in order to purchase book copies in bulk or to arrange for a speaking engagement, write to Mary Valloni at mary@fullyfundedacademy.com.

To the unsung heroes of mission fields worldwide whose faith, courage, and unwavering commitment inspire us all. To all missionaries who have ever felt alone.

To the first students of Fully Funded Academy, who believed there was a better way to raise money. You have given ministry workers around the globe the gift of going second.

Contents

What This Book Is, How to Use It, and the Lies Missionaries Tell Themselves

THE PRAYER FOR MISSIONARIES written by the Missionary Society of St. Columban reads: "O Sacred Heart of Jesus, Your missionaries have cheerfully left home and all dear to them for love of You and to bring Your love to Your poor. We beg You to strengthen that spirit of love in their souls. Let it never be weakened by failure, frustration, difficulty, or trial. Be with them in loneliness and hardship. Send them the help they need to carry on their work for You and make it fruitful for the salvation of souls."

Coming across this prayer felt like a "God moment" for us. Mary found it while sorting out a box belonging to her father shortly after he passed away. A card slipped out of one of his Bibles that had this prayer on it. Right around that time, she had decided to step away from her fundraising roles at a few globally known nonprofits to use her talents in order to help missionaries raise money. It was as if God was confirming her new direction. At the same time, God was doing some special things in Mike's life, and in chapter 1, you'll hear more about how our paths converged. To say it was unexpected and that we're a bit of an unlikely pair would be an understatement, but that's often how God works.

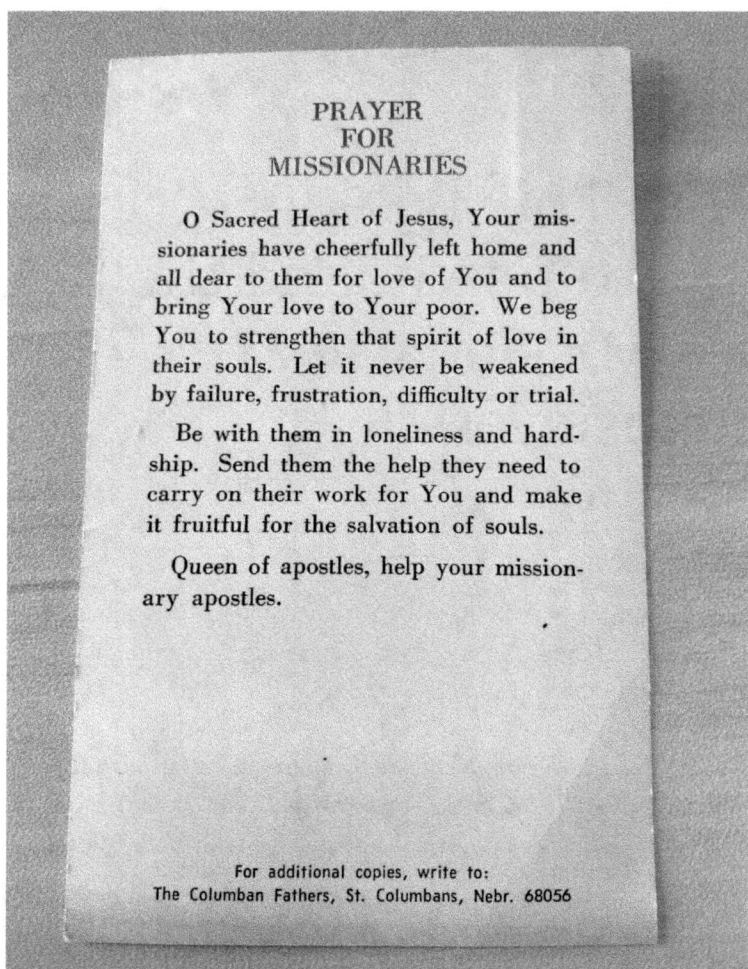

PRAYER
FOR
MISSIONARIES

O Sacred Heart of Jesus, Your missionaries have cheerfully left home and all dear to them for love of You and to bring Your love to Your poor. We beg You to strengthen that spirit of love in their souls. Let it never be weakened by failure, frustration, difficulty or trial.

Be with them in loneliness and hardship. Send them the help they need to carry on their work for You and make it fruitful for the salvation of souls.

Queen of apostles, help your missionary apostles.

For additional copies, write to:
The Columban Fathers, St. Columbans, Nebr. 68056

"Send them the help they need." That part of the prayer always jumps out at us. We can't help but think of the countless times over the years

when people would tell us, "The work you guys do is an answer to prayer. I prayed to God that He would send me help to raise this budget, and I found you online somehow."

We're always humbled when we get notes like this because it breaks our hearts that so many missionaries feel abandoned and alone. Missionaries don't get much love and appreciation, but we want you to know that *we* see and honor you. You carry a special place in our hearts. Both of our lives have been deeply impacted by missions, and we know that you carry a unique calling and pioneering spirit.

There's a saying, "Pioneers take the most arrows." It means that individuals who are the first to explore new places or do new things often face the most criticism and challenges. That said, we've found that some of the hardest challenges missionaries face aren't "in the field" but rather in raising the money needed to get on or stay there. That's why we're so excited you've picked up this book.

Everything we're going to share with you is based on this principle: *Do the difficult work of making things simple.* We're here to help you make it easier for supporters to understand who you are, what you do, why you do it, and why they should support you. In turn, we want to make raising support easier and more effective for you. Unfortunately, simplifying things isn't always easy. Habits and mindsets can be hard to change, so we humbly ask you to keep an open mind and heart. Some insights will be obvious, while others won't yield a "lightbulb moment" until weeks, months, or even years later.

Since 2018, we've helped thousands of missionaries through our program, Fully Funded Academy (FullyFundedAcademy.com). One of our members recently told us, "After months of hearing what you guys are saying, this *finally* makes sense. I've been looking at support raising all wrong!" We often get these kinds of comments.

Raising support in today's world requires a shift away from old habits and mindsets. Many of our members share that the training they've received is minimal, nonexistent, or irrelevant for the hyper-noisy online world we're currently living in. Some of the best-known books on raising support were published when email first hit the scene or when cell phones, social media, and video conferencing were almost nonexistent. In the past, face-to-face meetings, snail mail newsletters, phone calls, and speaking at churches helped many missionaries raise money. These can still be effective, but a lot has changed. Every day, your donors are operating within a society that makes things quick, easy, and efficient. We must adapt.

The things you'll learn here are field-tested in real-world fundraising. Tens of thousands of people have attended our free online trainings, and our Fully Funded Academy members have collectively raised millions of dollars. The material here has been refined over the years and has been battle-tested through economic ups and downs, including the pandemic in 2020. The principles here have worked and continue to work. Our prayer is that they'd work for you, too.

That said, this book isn't meant to be your only resource. We simply want to add a few more tools to your toolbox. Think of this book less like your latest read and more like a blueprint. Don't just read the book, "do" the book. At the end of each chapter, we'll provide some action items for you to move forward. Take action and refer back to it like any builder would refer to a blueprint. The main chapters are divided into seven steps using the word FREEDOM as an acronym:

1. Focus Your Vision
2. Run Your Research
3. Enlist Your Team
4. Enhance Your Brand
5. Deploy Your Team
6. Organize Your Ask
7. Make Your Difference

Chapters will be written by the person more suited to the topic. Mike will take the lead on chapters about messaging, and Mary will take the ones more closely tied to fundraising. The last three chapters will dive deeper into topics like writing a winning support letter, planning your year-end campaign, and hosting a fundraising event.

You'll also find templates, scripts, and other resources throughout the chapters. Download them for free at FullyFundedAcademy.com and use them liberally.

You Will Learn about Marketing, Psychology, and Storytelling (And You Should)

There's a saying, "Give a man a fish, and you feed him for a day. Teach a man to fish, and you feed him for a lifetime." We want to teach you to fish. We realize the words "marketing" and "psychology" can feel at odds with ministry. But in reality, all of us are engaged in some form of persuasion. As you study and implement the things we teach, your skills, competence, and awareness will grow. Not only will you become a better fundraiser, you'll become a more powerful communicator, storyteller, preacher, and leader.

You'll also see that while you may feel too small to raise a lot of money, the opposite may be true. In many ways, small is the new big. If you think about it, big corporate entities (including larger nonprofits and ministries) are spending billions of dollars to sound small, approachable, and personal. You already have the advantage they're trying to buy! We'll show you how to use your unique stories, personal touches, and thoughtful communication to create a bigger impact.

The Lies Missionaries Tell Themselves

While we've both spent considerable time studying Scripture and serving in vocational and volunteer roles in ministry, this book won't go deep on any kind of exegesis or theological study. (If it makes you feel any better, Mike went to seminary and earned a Master of Arts in Biblical Literature.) There are other incredible resources that go deeper into the theology of raising support. We won't attempt to convince you that raising support is biblical; rather we're going to assume you know that already. We'll also work under the assumption that you believe raising money in a biblical way is the right thing to do.

Yet we can't go further without acknowledging some of the challenges so many of the missionaries we've worked with have faced, especially around money. Many of these challenges are rooted in flat-out lies and can feel heavy and oppressive, as if you're standing at the door of a room full of dusty boxes. The boxes are stacked from floor to ceiling, and the clutter can be so overwhelming that light can barely shine through the windows. The whole thing feels dank, dark, and suffocating.

Friend, let's clear the room together and let the light shine through. Remind yourself of the beautiful day when God called you to ministry. Remember the joy and excitement that came when God spoke to you and you knew you were walking out His call on your life. The lies you've told yourself (or others have told you) about what missionary life "should" look like are over. We hope that today is the start of your new story.

Our missionary friends from Fully Funded Academy helped write this next section and titled it, "Lies Missionaries Tell Themselves." It's powerful! There's no better way to start this journey together than by hearing directly from people like you who have made some big shifts in the way they see fundraising, money, missions, and themselves. We encourage you to read through this list, discard the lies, and cling to the truth of the Scriptures.

1. Lie: God gave me a huge mission and then left me without funding.

Truth: Remember, God equips those He calls. It's about trusting His provision, which often unfolds through building relationships, sharing your mission, and embracing community support.

From Moses and Joshua's leadership transitions (Deuteronomy 31:7, Joshua 1:5) to David's counsel to Solomon (1 Chronicles 28:20) and Jesus's promise to His disciples (John 14:18), we see a constant theme of divine companionship. The writer of Hebrews (Hebrews 13:5–6) and Paul in his letters (1 Thessalonians 5:24, Romans 11:29) echo this assurance, reminding us that God's call and gifts are steadfast and irrevocable, guiding and providing for us at every step.

2. Lie: I was called to ministry, not to fundraise.

Truth: The talents you've honed for teaching and leading are the same ones you can use to build your support network. If raising funds feels foreign, it might be because it's an undeveloped skill or a mindset hurdle, especially if discussing money feels uncomfortable. Recognize that whether someone has significant resources or not, what we're really looking for is the heart to give. By not inviting them to support, we miss out on enabling them to exercise their God-given gifts. Proverbs 9:9 and the stories of Jesus calling the fishermen (Matthew 4:19, Mark 1:17) remind us that we're multifaceted with skills adaptable to various aspects of our mission, including fundraising.

3. Lie: I'm unequipped for this and all alone.

Truth: Many biblical heroes like Moses, Elijah, David, and Mary felt unequipped for their God-given missions, yet they weren't alone. God's guidance and companionship, alongside a supportive community, empowered them. Embrace your fundraising journey as an opportunity for growth, supported by the example of those who've gone before us and the community God provides.

4. Lie: My friends and family should automatically support my ministry financially.

Truth: Just as Jesus noted that a prophet is not honored in their own hometown (Mark 6:4), not every friend or family member may feel called to support your ministry financially. It's important to share your journey with them, and if they show interest, they may contribute. Value these relationships regardless of financial involvement.

5. Lie: If someone gives financially, I'm taking something away from them.

Truth: People have a natural desire to give. The act of giving is a spiritual gift, and we are all called to generosity. This isn't a zero-sum game. Inviting someone to support your ministry allows them to participate in God's work, offering them joy and fulfillment. Remember the widow's mite (Luke 21:1–4) and the feeding of the five thousand (Mark 6:30–44), where God's provision far exceeded human expectations. Giving allows both givers and receivers to experience God's generosity.

6. Lie: No one likes to fundraise. I don't like support raising so that must mean no one else does either.

Truth: While support raising may feel daunting, many find joy and purpose in it. Mary is one of them! Remember, fear often stems from the unfamiliar or skills we haven't yet mastered, including our approach to money.

The Bible speaks extensively about money, wealth, and possessions, with over 2,300 verses touching on these topics. It underscores the importance of our attitude toward money and generosity. For instance, the Macedonian church's giving during severe trials (2 Corinthians 8) exemplifies joy-fueled generosity born out of a deep commitment to the Lord and His people.

Paul's encouragement to the Corinthians (2 Corinthians 8:7) to excel in the grace of giving shows us that giving is a spiritual gift to be developed and cherished just like any other. This mindset shift transforms our approach to support raising from a task to be feared to a ministry opportunity to be embraced.

7. Lie: Asking should be easy if you're doing good work.

Truth: Fundraising isn't inherently easy, even for worthwhile causes. It's crucial to actively engage and communicate with potential donors, making the significance of your mission clear. Your work is important, but sharing its impact with others requires effort and relational engagement.

Engage with others as you would with a friend, sharing not just needs but also stories and updates that draw them closer to the heart of your ministry, as Paul did in his letters to the early churches.

8. Lie: If finances are there, it's God's plan. If not, then it isn't.

Truth: God's plan requires our active participation, including asking for support. Scripture encourages us to ask in faith for our needs and the needs of the ministry. In John 16:24, Jesus tells us, "Ask and you will receive, and your joy will be complete." This principle is echoed in the call for laborers in Matthew 9:37–38 and Luke 10:1–7, highlighting the necessity of both prayer and action in God's work. Furthermore, 1 Timothy 6:17–19 advises believers to trust in God's provision, encouraging generosity and stewardship. Financial challenges shouldn't deter us but rather motivate us to engage more deeply in faith and partnership with God and His community.

9. Lie: Missionaries should be poor.

Truth: God calls us to a life filled with His abundance, not scarcity. Jesus Himself stated in John 10:10 (ESV), "I came that they may have life and have it abundantly," emphasizing that this promise extends to everyone, including missionaries. It's crucial to navigate wisely between personal needs, community perceptions, and the impact of external funding on local dynamics. While the Bible shares examples like Paul learning contentment in every circumstance (Philippians 4:11–13) and Jesus's humble lifestyle (Luke 9:58), it also supports the notion that those who preach the gospel have a right to receive support (1 Corinthians 9:14). The aim isn't poverty for the sake of humility but living in a manner that aligns with God's provision and purpose for our ministries.

10. Lie: Missionaries should struggle or even suffer.

Truth: It's not God's will for missionaries to deliberately seek out suffering. Jesus, in Matthew 11:25 and 11:30 (ESV), reveals God's wisdom and offers rest to those who are burdened. This implies a life not designed for unnecessary hardship. While suffering is a part of life, intentionally adding to a missionary's struggles misrepresents God's calling. Jesus's ministry and Paul's teachings indicate that those serving in ministry should not be forced into poverty or hardship as a misguided attempt at humility or control. True biblical service is marked by a light burden and rest for the soul.

11. Lie: When missionaries say yes to ministry, they say no to all worldly possessions.

Truth: Accepting a ministry calling doesn't mean abandoning all material possessions. Paul speaks to being content regardless of circumstances and acknowledges the intentional hardships he faced to avoid hindering others' faith. However, he clearly supports the idea that ministers deserve fair compensation for their work, arguing for "double honor" for those who labor in preaching and teaching. This perspective shifts the focus from a vow of poverty to a balanced approach to possessions and financial support in ministry.

12. Lie: Raising money is a necessary evil.

Truth: Raising support is a way to invite others into worship through generosity. God provided for the Levites through the generosity of His people, showing that provision comes from communal support (2 Chronicles 31:4–8). Similarly, Jesus and his disciples were supported by followers (Luke 8:1–3), and Paul balanced earning income with accepting support, openly advocating for ministers' financial care (1 Timothy 5:17–18; 2 Corinthians 9:7).

13. Lie: A missionary's budget should only cover basic needs on the mission field.

Truth: God is generous and delights in fulfilling the desires of our hearts. A well-resourced missionary can better serve, anticipate unexpected challenges, and bless others. Sustainable ministry might require adapting to less than what's typical at home, yet it's crucial to be fully equipped. Discussing finances openly, regardless of the economic status of those involved, is part of effective ministry. Remember, the Levites were sustained by tithes, showing that God's provision for His servants is comprehensive and purposeful.

***

Powerful stuff, right? Big thanks to the missionaries who contributed to the above section. Their fingerprints are all over this book. We hope you've already felt a surge of hope and excitement, and we're thrilled to embark on this journey with you.

May this book be a guide that makes your work more effective and transformative. More than that, we hope it feels like you're talking warmly with two friends who really care about you and want to see you thrive because we do! Let's get started, friend.

Soli Deo gloria,
Mary Valloni and Mike Kim

CHAPTER 1

Focus Your Vision

I (Mike) spent a huge part of my youth and young adult life involved in church ministry. One of the perks was rubbing shoulders with leaders, some of whom were the best communicators I'd ever heard at that point in my life.

In those early years, I thought the ability and effectiveness of a speaker had more to do with their God-given anointing than anything else. They were just "gifted." Imagine my surprise upon learning that many of them spent hours crafting their messages and went so far as to rehearse their actual sermon in front of others before the weekend service.

One influential pastor told me that he intentionally asked non-Christians to sit in on his rehearsals to point out any references or illustrations they didn't understand. His goal was to communicate as clearly as possible to the greatest number of people and weed out any assumptions he might make about what his listeners would know. He shared the age-old adage, "A mist in the pulpit is a fog in the pew."

The Difference between Purpose, Vision, Mission, and Goals

One of the greatest gifts you can give your donors is clarity. To do that, you must focus your vision. I've always loved this acronym for the word "focus"--"Follow One Course Until Success."

Whenever we teach focusing your vision, folks get stuck because "vision" and other related words are often used interchangeably. It's easy to get hung up on the difference between purpose, mission, or vision. This can paralyze you from what you are ultimately trying to do, which is to paint a clear picture for potential donors to understand what you do and why they should consider supporting your work. For our purposes here, let's differentiate these concepts so we can move forward. Think of purpose, vision, mission, and goals like a hierarchy:

1. Purpose
2. Vision
3. Mission
4. Goals

When it comes to the *purpose* of our ministry (and lives), it's pretty simple: Glorify God. This is a wide enough umbrella to cover any and all things you'll do in ministry. The Westminster Catechism puts it well: "Man's chief end is to glorify God, and to enjoy Him forever." The purpose of your ministry, no matter what shape or form it takes, is to glorify God.

Vision is how you glorify God through your ministry. Will you plant a church? Will you be an evangelist? Will you provide for felt needs in a community? This may change with the different seasons of your life, but your purpose in life will never change.

Mission (which you should remember is a military term!) is a short-term campaign to help actualize the vision. Missions are characterized by parameters and measurables by which you can determine their success or failure. I have several friends who have served in the military, and they always say there is no such thing as a mission that does not have clear parameters. In the marketing world, the term "campaign" is used because there are clear parameters that define success for a marketing campaign.

Goals are the objectives, accomplishments, and mile markers by which you will measure a mission or campaign's progress.

These definitions, at least for the purposes of fundraising, will help us get on the same page throughout this book and prevent us from getting hung up on semantics. It's easy to waste time creating slogans or catchphrases rather than honing your skills or creating a real plan to raise the money you need. *You don't need a slogan; you need clarity.*

No More Christian Jargon

One of the first things we ask missionaries to do during our training sessions is to spell out their vision, mission, and goals. The only caveat: they're not allowed to use "Christianese"—our way of referring to Christian jargon.

Initially, folks often articulate their vision through phrases like, "To know Him and make Him known" or "His Kingdom come." Others just quote a Scripture verse or a derivative of it and claim that as their vision, such as building an "Acts 2 church" or fulfilling Matthew 28, the Great Commission.

None of these are wrong in principle. They just aren't helpful in helping others understand what you really do, especially if they don't know what is meant by an "Acts 2 church" or what Matthew 28 even says (and you shouldn't assume they do). Using jargon to cast vision is a crutch that can compound the challenge of raising more money. Why?

Because one of the greatest challenges you will face in getting (and staying) fully funded is widening your support base. If you don't expand your capability to communicate with people from different backgrounds or walks of life, you'll severely limit your options. Sure, many of your current and future donors will share your faith. But if you've ever visited a denomination or stream of ministry different from yours, you may have experienced how different even Christian jargon can be from one group to another.

For example, I grew up in a charismatic church where a prayer meeting meant gathering with others at church at 5 a.m. to pray loudly with a musician playing in the background and a prayer leader on a microphone. (Only later did I realize this was a pretty typical practice in Korean churches.) Imagine my surprise when attending a prayer meeting at a friend's Episcopal church. There was no music, no one leading the meeting, and people just sat in the church and prayed individually. This reminds me of the first time I visited the southern United States. I grew up in New Jersey, where we drink "soda." When I went to a local diner in Georgia, I didn't know what the waitress meant when she asked what kind of "pop" I wanted.

It's your responsibility to increase your ability to communicate with different people about your ministry. Mary and I are often asked how to connect with bigger donors, many of whom have built wealth and have the resources to give larger amounts. We'll cover this more in-depth later, but for now, consider this: Many of these "bigger donors" speak a different language day in and day out. If they own a business or work in leadership positions at their company, they're likely using clear, concise communication that often involves numbers and other metrics. That's the language they use to make decisions Monday through Friday at work.

If someone who is ready to donate a significant amount of money asks you what the goal for your ministry is for the coming year, you might need to have a better answer than "To know Him and make Him known." This is why we train our students to speak in terms that don't hide behind Christian jargon, Scripture verses, or slogans. Remember: *you don't need a slogan; you need clarity.*

Success Story: Dan Hurrelbrink in Romania

To put this all together, let's take an example from one of the missionaries we coached, Dan Hurrelbrink. We first met Dan in 2017 at our first in-person workshop. Based in Romania, Dan was on leave in the United States with his family. This was the first time in eight years that he and his wife, Maria, along with their eight children, had traveled to the United States. Dan's biggest priority at the time was fully funding his personal budget so he could focus his attention on building the ministry he and his wife planted: Barnabas Ministries Romania.

The purpose of Dan's life was to glorify God, and the *vision* was to do this by transforming lives in Romania. But we had to dig deeper. Eventually, we found out that his *mission* was to serve rural Romanian children and families through their after-school program, outreach activities, a children's camp, and a community center. (It's totally normal to have more than one mission in the same way a military would have more than one mission when operating in another country.) Understanding this allowed us to set *goals* with Dan by which we could measure his progress.

Just like many missionaries, Dan was sent out by his local church as a young Christian eager to do God's work. He spent decades with little to no fundraising resources and didn't have a plan to become fully funded. After our time together, he made a personal commitment to turn things around for his family and his ministry. Within twelve months, his personal budget was fully funded, he had new excitement and buy-in from his board of directors, hosted his first in-person fundraising event, and was building relationships with new donors to his ministry, all because we focused and communicated the vision, mission, and goals with clarity.

Dan's experience is a testament to how casting a clear vision can get you where you want to be. That clarity then trickles down into all other areas of your fundraising efforts. It allows you to set clear and compelling goals. Once you make a habit of doing this, the sky's the limit.

Let's look at one more example, this time outside of the ministry and fundraising space, to see how a focused vision can rally people and fuel a movement. The insights are pretty incredible.

Dr. Don Berwick and the 100,000 Lives Campaign

In 2004, Dr. Don Berwick was serving as the head of the Institute for Healthcare Improvement (IHI). At that time, medical malpractice was one of the top causes of death in the United States. It's wild to think that one of the leading causes of death in the country was due to medical practitioners simply making mistakes, so Dr. Berwick was determined to do something about it.

Later that year, Dr. Berwick stood in front of thousands of his colleagues at a convention and cast a vision to reduce medical malpractice over the next eighteen months. Harnessing the power of clear and compelling communication, he boldly said, "I think we should save 100,000 lives. I think we should do that by June 14, 2006. By 9 a.m."

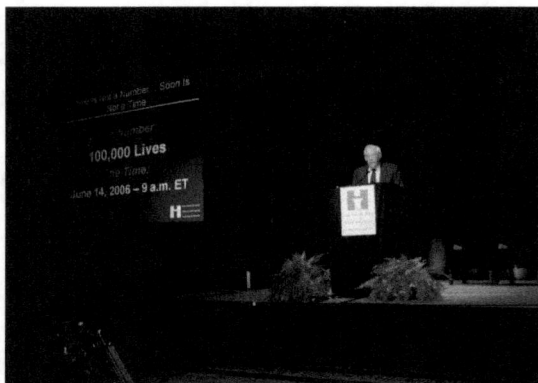

Now *that* is a clear and compelling vision! Notice what Dr. Berwick did *not* say. He did not say, "Let's reduce preventable harm in hospitals next year" or "Our vision is to reduce medical malpractice" or "Doctors, wash your hands." He used numbers, set a deadline, and sparked a movement. Dubbed the "100,000 Lives Campaign," Dr. Berwick and the IHI adopted the rallying cry "Some is not a number, soon is not a time"--and they ran full force to actualize this vision. Remember when I said earlier that marketers use the term "campaign" and set mission parameters? This is a great example.

The IHI defined six key interventions, including optimizing rapid response teams and preventing surgical site infections, pneumonia, and other adverse events. One of their goals was to enroll more than two thousand hospitals in the initiative. In the end, around 3,100 hospitals enrolled in the campaign—three-quarters of all hospitals in the United States at the time! On June 14, 2006, they celebrated more than 122,000 fewer needless deaths over the 18-month campaign period, and the 100,000 Lives Campaign eventually grew to become the 5 Million Lives Campaign.

Dr. Berwick's story illustrates the power found in the confluence of purpose, vision, mission, and goals. The purpose of a doctor is to save lives. Dr. Berwick's vision was to reduce medical malpractice. The mission was to save 100,000 lives by a certain date, and they set goals and initiatives that would support the mission's success.

I hope these examples give you a surge of hope and excitement. Just imagine the incredible things that could happen by taking some of these insights and applying them to your fundraising efforts.

Why You Should Talk about Your Ministry

All this talk of messaging, communication, and marketing can seem a bit unspiritual in the context of ministry, almost like trying to get oil and water to mix. At first glance, they seem like mutually exclusive concepts.

But here's what all of the missionaries and ministry leaders we've worked with confess: They don't want to come across as promotional or self-aggrandizing. They don't want to be seen as pushy, pestering, or, worst of all, prideful. To be labeled egocentric, arrogant, or even self-promoting is the one thing that most try to avoid at all costs.

As a result, some of us aren't very good at talking about our ministries. We hide behind the belief that all we need to do is pray that God will open doors, and doing anything more than that is trying to make things happen in our own power. We need a more balanced and healthy perspective. There is a middle ground between full-blown, self-promotional "celebrity" culture (which Mary and I personally don't like at all) and being completely silent and just "waiting on God." What if talking about your ministry involved you just doing what you can and God doing only what He can do? What if we've had the wrong "competitor" in mind this whole time?

Your Competitor Is the Enemy, Not Other Churches or Ministries

The enemy is shameless in vying for people's eyes, ears, hearts, minds, and souls. He will use any and every means necessary. *But your ministry is doing good things.* Please consider that there are people who could really use your help right this moment.

Perhaps you work with a team of translators to bring the Bible into a new dialect, you've written a great book that can help couples improve their marriage, or you planted an outpost that provides clean water for remote villages. Aren't these things people should know about? Think about that person in your city who will sleep outside in the cold tonight simply because they don't know about the shelter you built or the abuse victim who will take her own life because you never shared your story. Truly, the enemy is delighted that you'd rather not let people know about what you do.

Friend, you are uniquely qualified to meet a certain type of need in a very particular place for a certain type of person, and God has chosen you to do it. So why are we afraid to speak up and ask for financial support? Typically, we've found the reasons boil down to a handful:

- We're afraid of how people may view us.
- We're afraid people will reject us.
- We're afraid we might fail.
- We're afraid we might succeed!

All of the above boil down to the fear of man. We're not saying you should spam people and post a ton of things about your work on every social network all the time. But there are some best practices, so where do we start?

Start With Your (God-Given) Point of View

One of the amazing things about serving God is that while we all share the same purpose, He gives us different visions, gifts, talents, and passions. Vision starts with having your own point of view, so it's imperative that you dig deep inside of yourself.

To help draw out what's inside, I'm going to ask you three simple questions. I ask you for some grace here because I'm going to use language that will push the envelope a little bit. The reason is that I want to lean into the *emotions* behind what fuels you. This is just a starting point, so don't worry that you'll end up using this in your final fundraising materials. Just go with the flow and trust the process. The three questions are as follows:

1. What pisses you off?
2. What breaks your heart?
3. What's the big problem you're trying to solve?

The first question is about the *injustice* you see in the world. The second question is about the *compassion* you carry inside. The third question is the *vision* that fuels your ministry. The intersection of these three things is where your point of view is found:

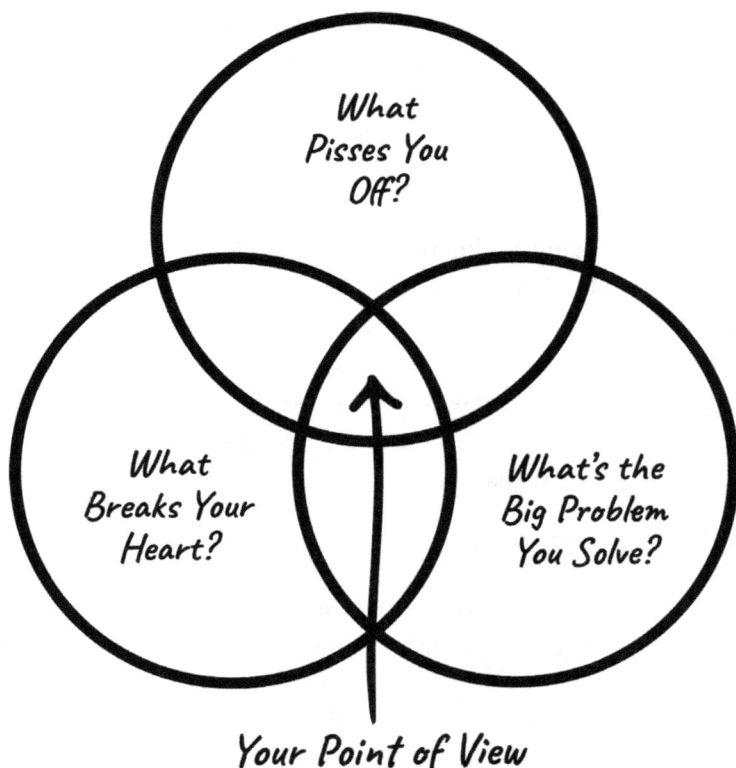

Remember, the first question, "What pisses you off?" addresses the injustice that you see in the world. This kind of language may not sit well with you, but it is intentional. If we simply ask you, "What is the injustice that you see in the world?" you'll likely respond with a very safe, watered-down answer. But if we ask you, "What pisses you off?," it can jolt you in a way that draws out the deeper emotions inside, similar to Jesus flipping tables in the temple. Of course, Jesus didn't always act with that level of intensity, but we want you to see that tapping into properly channeled emotions can be a good thing—especially when communicating your vision.

The second question, "What breaks your heart?" is the compassion that you have for people or a cause. We all know that without love, we're just a resounding gong and crashing cymbal. Anyone who only harps on injustice and what makes them angry becomes very noisy. But when you add compassion to the mix, love and justice meet.

The third question, "What's the big problem you're trying to solve?" draws out the vision of your ministry. Since this is backed by your answers to the first two questions, you're able to communicate the emotion and urgency of your calling in a more natural and effective way.

As an example, allow me to share a bit of how Mary and I met, why we wrote this book, and how our training program, Fully Funded Academy, got started. It was definitely a "God thing," but we also used the principles in this book to get the word out, help more people, and ultimately make a bigger impact. Hopefully, you'll see how natural and aligned it feels to use these questions to articulate your vision.

How Fully Funded Academy Started

Earlier, I mentioned that my young adult years were spent in church ministry. During my early thirties, I was serving full-time as a worship pastor at a Connecticut church and made many friends serving in missions both in the United States and abroad.

A few years later after I left that position, an old friend named Greg asked me for support. He and his wife were newly married and felt called to serve on the mission field. Greg and I spent a lot of time together during my ministry years. He often played drums when I was leading worship at events, and we recorded music together. I was happy to support him!

Little did I realize that sending him money would be so hard. Greg's sending organization preferred checks in the mail, and I hadn't owned a checkbook for years. When I went to his organization's website to donate, it required me to click through so many pages, buttons, and dropdown menus that I felt more like a computer hacker than someone trying to donate money. When I opted to simply wire him money directly, he said that wouldn't count toward the "official" amount he needed to be sent onto the field because it wasn't done through the organization. It was frustrating, to say the least. The organization was breaking one of the cardinal rules when it comes to fundraising: *Make it easy for people to give you money.*

The injustice I saw was that this young couple wasn't going to raise the money required to get on the field *for pointless reasons.* It broke my heart that this young couple would be kept on the sidelines. On top of making it hard for people to donate, his sending organization advocated for a "shake the trees" type of fundraising strategy for their missionaries, essentially training them to "churn and burn" through all their contacts in order to raise money. If anyone followed this strategy, it would result in a trail of burned relationships.

Around that time, I heard a statistic by the Narramore Christian Foundation that said about five thousand missionaries leave the field unnecessarily each year because of stress related to finances and personal issues. Five thousand! This truly broke my heart.

So, the big problem I set out to solve was to help missionaries improve their communication skills. Coming from a marketing background, there were valuable principles I could share. I hosted several free online trainings and wrote a blog post about how missionaries could raise more support. To my surprise, the blog post went viral and ranked on the first page of Google searches. A crush of new readers wanted to know more, so I hosted a few free online training sessions. By that time, I had stepped away from vocational ministry and had been running my own marketing consultancy, but I felt this was God's way of having me serve in ministry directly. I said, "God, I don't know what you want to do with this. This isn't even my main thing, but I'm really driven to help these people."

During that time, Mary was working on her first book, *Fundraising Freedom: 7 Steps to Build and Sustain Your Next Campaign*, which became the foundational steps to chapters in this book. Let's have Mary take it from here.

Mary: While writing my book, I was connected to a former pastor turned book coach named Kary. When I told Kary what my book was going to be about, he told me to connect with his friend, Mike Kim, because, on top of his own marketing business, Mike was helping missionaries raise money.

After doing some digging, I discovered that Mike had quite the following in the business space. He had a popular marketing podcast but was also writing blog posts about his work with missionaries. I took up the issue with God! I wasn't upset that Mike was helping missionaries get fully funded; I was upset Mike was helping missionaries get fully funded without me! I wanted to be a part of it!

I emailed Mike several times but never received a response. I figured it wasn't meant to be, so I put my focus on my upcoming book release. My book coach, Kary, hosted a conference in late 2017 where I was going to share the story of my book onstage. Wouldn't you know it: Mike was one of the guest speakers at this conference.

After Mike's session, I grabbed a copy of my book and introduced myself. To be honest, I was a bit annoyed with him for not returning my emails. I handed him my book and said, "Hi, I'm Mary Valloni." He responded, "Hey, I know who you are! You work with missionaries, right? Send me an email, and maybe we can do some stuff together." Wow, did he really just tell me to email him? I was about to strangle him! (Turns out I was emailing an account he never checks, and he was in between assistants, so things were slipping through the cracks.)

Anyway, I figured this was just Mike's way of politely saying "no," and I didn't think anything would come of this. I thought, "Why would Mike want to partner with me? He has his own thing going on," and I turned my attention to preparing for my session at the conference. I got to share the incredible journey I had been on for the past few years, which all began with the loss of my dad.

My father passed away from cancer in 2013, and within a few short months, my world flipped upside down. Nine months later, I resigned from my full-time position at the American Cancer Society to pursue my dream of helping missionaries, ministries, and start-up nonprofits raise money. After sharing my story at the conference, a man walked up to me during the break and began to prophesy that my work would impact generations to come and that I needed to be patient. He said, "God wants this to be an oak tree with strong roots that won't wither."

To my surprise, Mike tracked me down on the last day of the conference and asked for a few minutes to talk. The next thing I knew, he was scribbling down a strategy and timeline on how we could help missionaries together and asked if I wanted to partner with him. I wondered, "Is this really happening?" It was an out-of-body experience, and I still have a picture of what Mike drew.

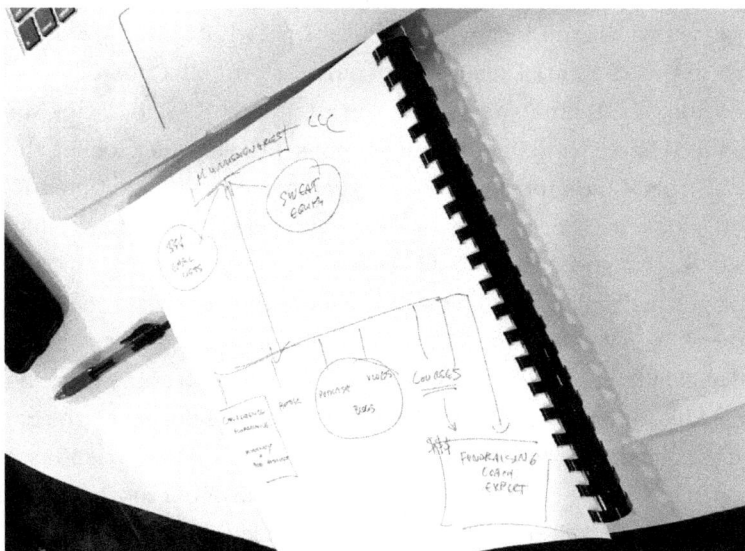

Later that day, I met up with some friends who all saw my meeting with Mike. They were freaking out because they knew my passion for missionaries and how talented Mike was. It all sank in while driving home the next morning. All the words that were prophesied over me just a day before seemed to come to life. The weight of them was just so overwhelming that I could barely breathe. I was trying to pack my bags and couldn't stop crying. I was pacing in my hotel, praying and thanking God, but also asking him, "Why me?"

Prepare for Your Moment

It's funny how we often cry out to God for new opportunities, yet when He opens doors, it's easy to feel unprepared or insufficient. A ton of thoughts ran through my head, "Was I ready? Could I handle this? Could I come close to matching what Mike had to bring to the table?" A friend called me during my drive and reminded me how hard I worked for this moment. He said, "You prepared for this moment, and this moment was prepared for you."

Just a few months later, we hosted our first in-person workshop (the same one in San Diego where we met Dan, whose story we shared earlier in this chapter). During one of our sessions, Mike shared his side of the story about how we met with the attendees. He said, "After Mary introduced herself and handed me her book, I took a quick look at the front and back and thought it looked great. After I had some time to myself, I looked at her website and knew she did things with excellence and knew what she was doing. That's really all it took."

That's really all it took, but it took a lot of time to create the content for my website and to work on that book! Yet, in just seconds, Mike made the decision to continue the conversation with me. After the workshop ended, Mike and I spent some time debriefing, and I dug up all the emails I sent that he never responded to. It was hilarious, and our friend Jason recorded the entire thing. Those videos are some of our most treasured memories. But in all seriousness, we both realized that God had done something really incredible by bringing us together.

Since 2017, we've trained thousands of missionaries, hosted numerous workshops both in-person and online, expanded our reach to train ministry organizations, and, most importantly, have helped more people get fully funded so they can serve the people God has called them to serve. One of our members, Lydia Nigh, serving with a global missions organization, wrote:

> *Two years ago, my husband had a heart attack, and I wondered how I'd financially survive if he died. My nineteen-year-old working at the movie theater was making more than me. I jumped on a Fully Funded training. Two years later, I have gone from being beaten up and discouraged to being lifted up and cheered on, to finally crossing the line. A donor received a financial blessing and texted me. "How much more do you need?" They picked up my remaining deficit, and now I am fully funded!*
>
> *Fully Funded Academy has deeply impacted how I view support raising. I had ongoing encouragement to consistently pursue and love people and to clearly share my vision and invite them to it. Thank you to Mary, Mike, and the amazing Fully Funded Academy community!*

The Vision Is Always Bigger Than You

We love what Lydia said in her remarks above: "consistently hold up my vision and invite them to it." As we close this chapter, we want to remind you that the vision God has placed inside your heart is (and should be) way bigger than you. Our prayer is that you have more than enough money for every endeavor, project, and initiative in your heart.

The clarity we have behind *Fully Funded* has allowed us to share our vision with team members, colleagues, friends, and, most importantly, with the people we want to directly serve. We urge you to take the time to answer these three simple questions:

1. What pisses you off?
2. What breaks your heart?
3. What's the big problem you're trying to solve?

Don't hold back. Don't filter yourself. Draw the emotions out and get it down on paper. Once you do, you'll be able to continue focusing your vision and refining your message. In the next chapter, we'll look at more real-life examples of missionaries and ministry leaders we've worked with who have experienced tremendous transformation in their fundraising. You'll benefit from their insights and real-life success stories, so turn the page after you've answered the three questions and let's dive in.

***

At the end of each chapter, we'll list some action items to help you apply the ideas discussed. We've also put these exercises in a convenient workbook that contains all the exercises for the rest of the book, which you can download free at FullyFundedAcademy. com.

1. Take a moment to write down your Vision, Mission, and Goals as best you can.
2. Answer the question, "What pisses you off?" In other words, what is the injustice you see in the world?
3. Answer the question, "What breaks your heart?"
4. Answer the question, "What is the big problem you're trying to solve through your ministry?"
5. What did you notice in your answers to the above questions? Did you have any takeaways or insights?

CHAPTER 2

Run Your Research

When I (Mary) worked at the American Cancer Society, it was my job to launch several fundraising campaigns throughout the year. Organizations like the American Cancer Society don't get that large and influential overnight; they get there by having a clear purpose, vision, mission, and goals.

Despite the American Cancer Society's success decade after decade, my mentor, John Kyger, would always say to me, "Mary, go do your Sherlock Holmes research and come back to me." In other words, he was telling me to *run my research* before doing anything. This is the same charge I want to pass on to you right now.

Part of the reason I encourage you to do this is because so many missionaries feel alone. When Mike and I teamed up to host free online classes shortly after we met, we didn't anticipate the kind of emotions people were experiencing on the calls. As people shared the stories of how they were called into a particular field or part of the world, tears flowed freely. Folks were incredibly generous and willing to share what was working for them in their fundraising efforts. They were quick to encourage others. We would pray together, and you could feel the pleasure in God's heart as we gathered. It was a true snapshot of the larger body of Christ.

For many, these calls were the first time they truly felt seen and understood. They weren't alone or isolated anymore. Many would say, "Wow, I had no idea there were so many of us!" Missionaries can be a different breed: You're unconventional, adventurous, on-the-edge kind of folks. You're entrepreneurial in many ways, seeing opportunities that others don't see and driven by a vision that has yet to materialize. And that's exactly why you need to connect with and learn from others like you!

When I started my business as a fundraising consultant, one of the people I admired most at the time was my mentor, John. His decades of fundraising experience and oversight of a huge staff showed me what true leadership looked like. He was so passionate about his work. He set high standards. He advocated hard for the people he served. Most importantly, he loved his team. As a result, John's life served as a model for me to follow.

Embrace Radical Humility

Part of the reason Mike and I are so passionate about bringing missionaries together is that many of them don't know other people who are raising funds *well*––but they are out there! Success leaves clues, so if you can put on your own Sherlock Holmes hat and study what others are doing, you set yourself up to grow and get better results. This will require some outreach, but it will be worth it:

1. Find three individuals who are fully funded.
2. Follow their work by observing what they post online or by joining their email list.
3. Ask each person to have a one-on-one conversation with you.

Doing this will require you to embrace radical humility. Asking for help is not a sign of weakness but rather a sign of growth and maturity! If you're not an expert in a specific area, there's no honor in trying to fake it or in paying the so-called "dummy tax"—especially when it comes to something as important as raising support. Stay teachable and learn from those who have more experience and better results than you. Just like we saw during our online training calls, you'll find that people are more likely to share insights with you than you might think.

Below is a simple email script you can send to these individuals. Before you do, truly take the time to observe what they do first and then reach out. People can sniff out a phony message from a mile away! Here's a quick template you can take and tweak:

***

Dear [Name],

My name is [Your name]. I found you by word of [how you found them] and love your work!

I am preparing to go into mission work in [Location] with [Name of ministry] and was wondering if you'd be open to sharing some of the insights you've gained in raising support. I've just started my support raising journey and really admire how you do things.

Would you be open to a brief call (20–30 minutes) in the next week or two? If so, here are a few options:

[Date] at [Time]

[Date] at [Time]

[Date] at [Time]

If these times don't work for you, I'm more than happy to work around your schedule. I would be so grateful!

Would you be open to a brief call?

Sincerely,

[Your name]

***

If you don't hear back, try not to take it personally. Like you, they're probably busy, or perhaps they just don't check their communication channels regularly like Mike when he and I first met! If you get a hard and fast "no," then just trust that God has someone else you can learn from.

Success Story: Christian and Hannah Swails

Christian and Hannah Swails were in their twenties, newly married, and felt the call to full-time ministry on the mission field. A year later, they started to raise support but found that much of the training was outdated. "There wasn't a lot of literature on this," says Christian. "There wasn't a lot of legitimate training, especially for the age of internet and social media."

After three long years of trying to raise support, the Swails only reached 60 percent of their total funding. They heard about our workshop (yep, the first one we hosted in San Diego) but wrestled with the idea of attending. Christian says, "I thought, is this a selfish thing? I want to go hang out in San Diego for a couple days and get some cool training, too. We didn't have the extra funds, but I felt like the Holy Spirit saying this is something He wanted us to do."

One of the things we encourage missionaries to do is to make a direct ask from supporters to fund their training and development. Mike wrote this email template to help you do exactly that:

***

SUBJECT: I'd love to get your advice / help on...

Dear [first name of recipient],

One of our goals in 20xx and beyond is to create a sustainable plan for the ongoing work we're doing in [location where you serve].

That means clarifying our message, growing our donor base, and raising more support so we can help the people we serve.

It's a dream of mine to enroll in a support-raising training called Fully Funded Academy (FullyFundedAcademy.com) hosted by two fundraising and marketing professionals: Mary Valloni and Mike Kim.

Mike and Mary have worked with ministries like Catalyst, MOPS, People of the Second Chance, and nonprofits like the American Cancer Society and the Special Olympics.

This training is specifically for Christian missionaries, and it's a dream of mine to enroll so I can gain important skills that can improve the effectiveness of our ministry.

Recently, I joined Mary and Mike in a free support-raising training, and it was incredibly helpful. I can only imagine what more I'll learn if I join them inside Fully Funded Academy.

I've been going it alone for too long and really need some strong coaches to surround me in this particular area of the ministry.

Would you consider sponsoring my enrollment?

The investment is $___ a month or just $___ for the year.

Fully Funded Academy promises to be of tremendous help to the ministry, and it would also give me the chance to rub shoulders with other co-laborers in Christ.

Would you help make this dream a reality?

If you're willing, please send a quick reply to this email! Or feel free to text or call me at [YOUR PHONE NUMBER].

It would mean so much to me and the people I serve if you are willing to help make this dream come true.

Thank you!

In Christ,

[YOUR NAME]

***

After sending this out, Christian and Hannah received a gift for the exact amount for their enrollment from a supporter they hadn't heard from in those three years. After spending a few days around other missionaries, they started to overcome their scarcity mindset. Their confidence in what God called them to do grew, and over lunch, they started using phrases like "We're gonna be" and "We're going to." Hannah started to say, "I am a missionary," and began to own it.

It's so easy to talk about a far-away future where everything is in "the next chapter." But just because you aren't on the field yet doesn't mean you aren't already walking in your calling. "That was super eye-opening," says Christian. "This is the season that God has us in right now—to teach us things He wants us to learn. But this is very much a part of our journey of currently being missionaries."

After three years of laboring hard to raise just 60 percent of what they needed, Christian and Hannah raised more than the remaining 40 percent within just eight weeks after the workshop. They were *over* 100% fully funded and found themselves packing to move to and minister in Spain that very summer.

"We not only had the training you guys gave us but a community that built on all the support behind us. We were meant to live in community. When you're with other people, it bonds you and gives you a support system that enables you to continue forward."

Christian and Hannah didn't have any models of fully funded missionaries in their immediate circles, so they ran their research on the new friends they made inside Fully Funded Academy. They focused their vision and built a team (which we'll cover in the next chapter), and as a result, entire groups of people are now hearing the gospel in Spain.

Just a quick note: While we love that someone swooped in to support Christian and Hannah for a last-minute opportunity, this isn't a long-term strategy. God can send us gifts and surprises, but there's also a flip side. We're told over and over again in Scripture to prepare and make plans, and that's exactly why we want you to research others.

Research Possible Donors

While it's important to run your research so you can model your fundraising efforts after those who have been successful, it's equally important to run your research on potential donors.

We can't close this chapter without telling you about some of the worst ways you can try to raise support. We've seen far too many missionaries and ministry leaders burn bridges and ruin relationships because they were taught "a churn and burn" approach to raising support as if your family, friends, and social media connections are a list of prospects to tear through and hit up for money.

Maybe this approach worked a few decades ago, but we live in a hyper-connected world now through the internet and social media. The way people connect and communicate with each other has changed. To be fair, the missionaries we've met do not want to raise support this way. They've just been taught (and, in many instances, *forced*) to do so by their sending organizations. As a result, they have an aversion to fundraising. Over the years, we've polled thousands of them, and the most common reasons boil down to these few statements:

- I feel icky asking for money.
- I only talk to people when I need money, and it feels like I'm using them.
- I've been taught to "shake the trees," and I feel like a salesperson, or worse, a beggar.
- I don't even know what to say when I reach out.
- Raising support feels like a necessary evil.

Let's take the flip side of these statements from the perspective of a potential donor. In what world would a person only want to be contacted when someone needs money? Especially if that person hasn't talked to them in months or years? And in what world would a person who knows little to nothing about you or your ministry donate their hard-earned money? The answer: not *this* world.

Unfortunately, much of the fundraising training that missionaries still receive today isn't that different from the tactics of a slimy, pushy salesman or a telemarketer who spams your phone. As a result, many Christians refuse to support missionaries, yet sending organizations keep pushing the same tactics and strategies.

Worse, decades of this type of training have bred a sense of entitlement in some missionaries that borders on pride and self-importance. They feel entitled to financial support and believe people should just give out of obligation or duty. Being in the ministry and nonprofit world, I'm often contacted by people asking for support. Every few weeks, I get a message like this (this is a real message):

"Hey Mary, I just want to tell you a little bit about my ministry. Let's get together. I'd love to jump on a call and talk to you about the work that I'm doing."

Most of the time, this is a person I haven't talked to in years. They might as well say, "Hey, I know we haven't talked in ten years, but now that I'm raising money, I want to talk about myself long enough for you to write me a check." To them, I'm not Mary; I'm a dollar sign.

Let me remind you: The people you're contacting are *your* relationships, not your sending organization's. These are *your* friends, your family, and your contacts. Your name is on the line, not someone else's. Take the time to run a bit of research before you blindly reach out. In this sense, social media can be a good thing. Every day, people post things that give insight into their passions, interests, or what's going on in their lives.

For example, a quick look at Mike's social media will make it very clear that he travels a lot, likes personal development books, enjoys spending time with his two young nephews, and that he has a really cute dog. (I'm starting to sound like a stalker, I know.) But all of these details are conversational touch points and serve as an easy on-ramp to talk to him.

What if, for example, I saw that Mike was visiting Washington, DC to see his nephews and I had a good restaurant or museum recommendation for them to go to? He might comment back on one of those posts, "Mary! Wow, it's been a long time! Great to hear from you. Thanks for the recommendation!"

Then he may check out my social media page to see what I've been up to (now he's the stalker!) and see that I'm doing some ministry work. He might comment on my page, and we might directly message each other to catch up. Obviously, this isn't going to happen in every scenario, but it's way better than the message I got above.

This isn't a hard and fast rule, but we've seen this countless times with the missionaries we coach: "Ask for money, get advice. Ask for advice, get money."

If the first thing you ask for is money, you'll often just get advice (or no response at all). If you reach out and only ask for money, it signals that you aren't really interested in truly connecting and that the relationship you're looking for is mostly transactional. It's also a clear tell that you have poor stewardship of both money and relationships, which is exactly why a "churn and burn" strategy is being used in this day and age. Very few people wake up and say, "I hope someone contacts me out of the blue and asks me for money today!"

If any of the folks who reached out to me had taken two minutes to scan my social media posts, they'd see that I could help them in bigger ways than a $50 monthly gift. Imagine if someone wrote to me asking for advice. "Hey Mary, I saw that you help nonprofit and ministry leaders raise more money. Could I run some ideas by you?" The value I could give them could be so much greater, and I'd probably support them financially with no hesitation because we'd be connecting on a deeper level.

When you run a little bit of research on your potential donors, you might find more than just a few monthly donors in your network. You might find multipliers, people who have vast connections or access to bigger opportunities and funds.

In the next chapter, we'll dive into the single most important driver to getting you fully funded. Every single missionary (100 percent!) who has done what we teach in the next chapter has been fully funded: enlist your team.

***

This chapter's homework is simple:

1. Find three individuals who are fully funded.
2. Follow their work by observing what they post online or by joining their email list.
3. Ask each person to have a one-on-one conversation with you using the template provided.

Remember, we've put these exercises in a convenient downloadable workbook, which you can download for free at FullyFundedAcademy.com.

CHAPTER 3
Enlist Your Team

Does your budget drive your vision, or does your vision drive your budget? It's a simple question with profound ramifications. If the budget is the driver, then you might need a bigger vision (ouch). If the vision is the driver, you'll probably need more money. To do that, you'll need a team.

Enlisting a team is the single biggest difference-maker for every person we've coached to get fully funded. It can also be the hardest step. Enlisting a team requires you to come face-to-face with your own self-limiting beliefs and step into a new level of leadership. You'll need to give up a measure of micro-managing and control. Your mindset will need to grow, as will your communication skills. But those who enlist the right team get and stay fully funded. Those who do not continue to struggle.

Enlisting a team isn't just for big organizations. It's for you, whether you're raising individual support, as a couple, or as a family. It's for you if you have a smaller ministry or if you've yet to even raise support. It's for you if you've been raising support for years. Missionaries often tell us that their contacts have "dried up"–that their connections have been exhausted, and they're not sure who to ask for support. Typically, these missionaries are busy and often away from home, so they don't have the ability to create or nurture new connections. Before long, supporters drop off, and they run out of money.

But if you have a team, your network is always growing. You're no longer carrying the burden of raising support by yourself. You have people who are actively praying for and participating in the work you do. Key word: *participating.*

When we look at the ministry of Jesus, we see that he only operated on his own for a very brief period of time. He may have started out in the wilderness by himself, but it didn't take long before he set out to enlist a team.

- Jesus was baptized (Matthew 3:13–17).
- Jesus was "alone" and tested (Matthew 4:1–11).
- Jesus began to preach "alone" (Matthew 4:17).
- He enlisted his team (Matthew 4:18–22).
- He reached the masses—his name spread throughout all of Syria. Great crowds followed him (Matthew 4:23–25).
- Jesus instructed the disciples (Matthew 5–9).
- Jesus is risen and he gives the Great Commission (Matthew 28:16–20).

If Jesus had to enlist a team, so will you. Effective fundraising is not a solo sport. No one person is great at every single thing that needs to be done in order to raise financial support. Both Mike and I have run our own businesses for years, and we often talk about our primary role in each of our respective endeavors. We've experienced the pain and burnout that can come so easily from doing everything alone. I love the perspective he shared with me recently. He said that as the founder and CEO of his organization, he has three jobs:

1. Cast vision
2. Remove friction
3. Build bridges

Keep this on your whiteboard, workstation, and even your refrigerator if you have to! To move to another level of freedom in your fundraising, you must focus on doing these three things. We've covered quite a bit about vision in the first chapter.

Removing friction is where a great many fundraisers suffer because, more often than not, we are our own bottleneck. Even if you're just raising personal support, we encourage you to have the same mindset an organization would. The single biggest mindset shift you can make in enlisting a team is to understand that you are the coach, not the player. Like the coach of any successful sports team, you'll have a say in who is playing, their role on the team, and the overall game plan. Together, you can achieve great things.

First Steps

There are five simple steps to get started. This process may stretch you, but remember, you're driven by a bigger vision than your own discomfort! If embraced, this can be an enjoyable and fruitful experience:

1. Create a Team Document
2. Enlist your team leader
3. Enlist other team members
4. Schedule your first team meeting
5. Host your first team meeting

When you ask someone to join your team, most people won't really know what you're asking them to do. They'll have all sorts of questions rolling around in their mind about the time commitment, financial commitment, or what their responsibilities will be. Some will wonder if they even have the skills or qualifications. This is where a Team Document comes in––an easy-to-read document that clearly outlines your team's roles, goals, and responsibilities. Start by explaining the purpose of the team using this template:

> *The (Team Name) Advisory Group is comprised of individuals, ministry, and community leaders who believe in the mission of (Missionary Name). The vision of (Team Name) is not to serve as a governing board but rather to promote and support the success of (Ministry). In doing so, this group will be assisting (Missionary Name's) mission to (add mission) and vision to (add vision).*

Here is an example:

> *The Johnson Advisory Team is comprised of individuals, ministry, and community leaders who believe in the mission of John and Sue Johnson. The vision of the Johnson Advisory Team is not to serve as a governing board but rather to promote and support the success of the Johnsons' work through Hope Ministries in Munich, Germany. In doing so, this group will be assisting John and Sue's mission to bring the gospel to the unreached through 100 home churches throughout Germany, France, and Spain by December 31, 20xx.*

This statement should sit at the very top of your Team Document. You can use anything for your team name--don't get caught up in the title. Some of our students have used terms like ministry team, support raising team, council, advocacy group, or advisory group. Go with whatever you feel comfortable with.

The next section should be a simple bullet point list with the expectations for members of this advisory group:

- Serve as a support system to [your team name].
- Attend three to four quarterly meetings through video conference or in person.
- Accept a "Give or Get Goal" of $____ in monthly or $____ annual support through one or more of the following avenues:
  - Securing a corporate monthly or annual gift
  - Securing a church monthly or annual gift
  - Making a personal monthly or annual contribution
- Host a fundraising event in your home, church, or business.
- Invite other businesses, churches, or personal contacts to donate.
- Allow the use of your name or company affiliation to promote and publicize [your team name].
- Invite friends, family, and contacts to support [your team name] movement.

All this information should fit on just one page. Take a look at this example created by one of our Fully Funded Academy members, Emily

Houser, for her organization, the Smoky Mountain Dream Center:

Smoky Mountain Dream Center Legacy Council

The Smoky Mountain Dream Center Legacy Council is comprised of individuals and groups who believe in the mission of Smoky Mountain Dream Center. The vision of the Legacy Council is not to serve as a governing board, but rather to promote and support the Smoky Mountain Dream Center to ensure every woman and child in Appalachia would have the opportunity to find **FREEDOM** from poverty, abuse and incarceration, **FLOURISH** in their homes, schools, work and community, and **FLY** towards the dreams God has placed on their hearts.

What does it mean to be a member of the Legacy Council?

- Serve as a support system to Smoky Mountain Dream Center
- Attend 3-4 quarterly meetings through video conference or in person.
- Accept a fundraising goal to give or get $10,000 in annual support through one or more of the following avenues:
  - Corporate monthly or annual gift
  - Church monthly or annual gift
  - A personal monthly or annual contribution
  - Host an event in your home, church or business
  - Invite other business, church or personal contacts to give
- Allow the use of your name, business or church affiliation to promote and publicize Smoky Mountain Dream Center
- Invite friends, family and contacts to support Smoky Mountain Dream Center

Benefits to being a member of the Legacy Council:

- Ability to use your skills and talent to advance the Kingdom.
- Priority access to send a team to the Smoky Mountain Dream Center for a future service project.
- Opportunity to speak and connect with the women and children in Appalachia with the opportunity to personally impact their lives.
- Direct access to the leadership of Smoky Mountain Dream Center as a speaker to share the impact of the ministry to your team, family, friends, congregation, etc.

These are very clear commitments. It's vital to ask each person or couple on your team to accept a minimum fundraising goal in monthly or annual support. Let's say you have four team members and you need $2,000 in monthly contributions. Simply ask team members to each raise $500 in monthly support (or $6,000 per year, which is $500 x 12 months). We call this a "Give or Get Goal"--either give $500 per month or raise $500 per month. In many instances, team members will donate the minimum amount themselves and happily go out and raise more support on your behalf.

Giving people responsibility breeds responsible people. In the last chapter, we mentioned Christian and Hannah Swails, who got fully funded just a few months after applying the principles we teach. Christian and Hannah focused their vision and built a team. Their team members were proud to be on Team Swails, and several of them persuaded people who didn't even know Christian and Hannah to support their work.

You might be nervous about asking team members to "give or get," but the money isn't typically their primary concern. They're usually more worried about the number of meetings they have to attend or the other time commitments involved in being on your team. If they've agreed to be on your team, don't shy away from setting a "Give or Get Goal."

Now, let's talk about recruiting your first team member.

What to Look for in Team Members

I often hear missionaries say, "I don't know anyone who would want to give to my cause or be on my team. I don't even know where to start." Let's shift to an optimistic and faith-filled perspective. Many of us have an amazing ability to talk ourselves out of approaching people who would be perfect for the task at hand. If you approach building a team with a negative expectation, you will only set yourself up to experience a self-fulfilling prophecy. Rather than making this a huge, overwhelming task, let's start small. *Let's start with one.*

The first person to look for is your team leader. Duties aside, let's first think through the kind of person you want to build your team around. The challenge is that this person won't know you're looking for them. Most people assume that all that's expected of them is to send money and aren't aware they can get involved in a bigger way.

The enlisting process goes both ways. Just as you are looking for a strong leader, the right individual will be looking for a strong leader in you--if they're asked. List the characteristics you should be looking for in your team leader. Don't overcomplicate it, but don't lower the bar either. Here are just a few to pull from:

- Godly character
- Well-respected
- Upbeat, positive, great to be around
- "Comes with their own batteries" (e.g., possesses a strong drive)
- Compassionate, empathetic
- Exhibits emotional and relational intelligence
- Effective communicator
- Track record of success
- Aligns personal values with your ministry ethos
- Capable of making personal and/or corporate financial contributions
- Possesses a strong network
- Possesses relevant professional skills
- Committed to ongoing personal and professional development
- Available to invest time, possibly due to a recent life change (e.g., children leaving home, retirement)

I know, I know. This person sounds like a unicorn, and unicorns don't exist! I assure you, this person is out there. In the same way that you cast a vision for your ministry, cast a vision for the kind of people you want on your team. One of the factors on the list above that you shouldn't overlook: Those who are available to invest time, possibly due to a recent life change. Some of the best team leaders among our members are folks who have retired from a robust corporate or business background and want to contribute to something closer to their faith. They may view this season of life as their opportunity to really pour into ministry in a more direct way.

Follow the same process for your other team members. Every strong organizational team has some blend of the following:

- Storyteller
- Designer
- Builder
- Dreamer
- Mentor

- Recruiter
- Connector
- Negotiator
- Teacher
- Salesperson
- Scientist
- Futurist
- Mathematician

There are a myriad of resources out there on how to build a team, but the emphasis here is to make sure you build things in a way that takes things off your plate and allows you to focus on what you do best. (While a business title, one book to consider reading is *Buy Back Your Time* by Dan Martell.)

Finally, don't overlook the power that is found in bringing people together. Imagine the potential connections that can happen when team members from various locations, churches, or backgrounds who have never met are brought together. You're expanding their network, not just yours, and for many, this is a key factor in why they decide to serve and stay involved.

How to Reach Out

When you recruit a team leader or members, please don't do this through email, text, or social media. This is a very personal and relational request, so take the time to call or do a video call. Let them hear your voice, see your face, and feel your energy. Let them know how serious this is. Let them know you are trying to take things to the next level so more people can be impacted for Christ and that they have been carefully considered for this role. You could say something like:

> *[Name], I'm thrilled that we are talking, and I really appreciate your time. You may already know about the big dreams and vision we have at [your ministry]. For the past few years, I've been trying to raise funds alone, but now I see the value in having a team, just like Jesus had his disciples. I've noticed your skills and how wonderfully you manage your business and family, and I deeply respect that. I would be honored if you'd consider joining our team.*

In response, they may inquire about what being part of the team entails. This is your opportunity to present your Team Document. It's crucial to have this document ready beforehand. The details aren't set in stone, but you want it as close to the final version as possible while still being flexible to changes. Now you can confidently say, "I've put together this simple team document that outlines everything. Can I share it with you?"

Just imagine how impressive this will sound to someone who has only heard from missionaries when they need money!

Walk them through the Team Document, making sure to communicate how soon you need the money raised. This timeframe will guide the frequency of your meetings, whether it's bi-weekly, monthly, or quarterly. Acknowledge the value of their time, but don't apologize for the commitment you're asking for.

When discussing the Give or Get Goal, shed some light on the size of your team and the monthly support goal. You might say, "We're aiming for a team of three to five members and would love your input on this. With five members and a $2,000 monthly goal, it breaks down to each member being responsible for raising about $400 a month. This is a Give or Get Goal, meaning you can help raise this money or give the amount yourself. We have several ideas on how this can get done."

Make sure to set clear expectations on what you're permitted to share regarding their involvement. Having team members willing to share about their involvement is a big part of rallying others to support you. Simply ask, "We'd be thrilled to feature you as a team member and share why you've decided to be part of this journey. Is this okay?"

Emphasize their role in the vision. You could say something like, "Joining our team offers a unique opportunity to leave a lasting legacy and profoundly impact lives. Your insights will be invaluable. Together, we have the chance to make a lasting difference, to change lives for the better. That's the heart of our mission, and that's why I believe you'd be an incredible addition to our team."

Remember, this is a significant commitment, so encourage them to take their time. "Please, don't feel rushed to decide today. Discuss it with your loved ones and pray about it. We want you to be fully committed and at peace with your decision."

Tailor all of this to your comfort level and the relationship you already have with the person. If they've been a supporter of your ministry, this conversation should flow naturally.

What if they say no? Don't be discouraged! It's important to have team members who are fully committed and enthusiastic about joining you. If they feel that this isn't the right time, express your understanding and keep the door open for the future. You can say something like, "Thanks for your consideration. I get that life is full of commitments, and if now isn't the right time, that's alright. We have immense respect and affection for you and your family."

Schedule Your First Team Meeting

If someone agrees to be part of your team, congratulations! If you still need more time to round up more members, just be upfront about the approximate timeline for how much more time it will be until you host your first team meeting. You want to err on the side of doing this quicker so you can use the momentum and excitement to kick things off in strength.

Your first meeting should include your entire team. Decide on the meeting format, whether it will be in-person, via video, or a phone call, carefully considering different locations and time zones. Offer a range of possible meeting dates and ask for their preference—do they find daytime, evenings, or weekends more convenient? This helps you gauge the best times to schedule future meetings as you coordinate with the rest of your team. As of this writing, we've found these tools to be helpful:

- **Doodle.com:** A web-based poll that makes it easy for participants to vote on their available meeting times
- **TimeAndDate.com:** Meeting time planner and other tools to coordinate different time zones
- **Zoom.us:** Video conferencing toolFor more up-to-date resources and a full list of tools our members have found helpful, visit FullyFundedAcademy.com/tools.

Host Your First Team Meeting

The first meeting is crucial for setting the tone and direction. Always have an agenda to keep the meeting on track. Here's a sample agenda that many of our members have used as a starting point. Feel free to take and tweak this to your liking:

- **Welcome and Introductions**
  - Start with a friendly greeting
  - Facilitate introductions, allowing each member to share about themselves
  - Encourage team members to talk about why they joined
- **Ministry Update**
  - Share recent developments and the current impact of the ministry
  - Discuss the progress made in your journey so far
- **Financial Overview**
  - Discuss monthly contribution goals
  - Be transparent about overall financial targets and what hitting those targets will allow the ministry to accomplish
- **Wish List of Key Contacts**
  - Share a list of desired contacts or supporters your team can help you connect with
  - Explore how team members can facilitate these connections
- **Action Item Assignments**
  - Assign specific tasks with clear deadlines to team members
  - Ensure clarity on who is responsible for each task
- **Next Meeting Planning**
  - Set the date and time for the next meeting
  - Outline the primary focus or objectives for the upcoming meeting
- **Feedback and Open Discussion**
  - Allow time for team members to give feedback or raise any concerns
  - Encourage open discussion to foster team cohesion and

collaboration

- **Closing Remarks**
  - End with a positive note, reinforcing the importance of everyone's contribution
  - Express gratitude for the team's involvement and commitment

In future meetings, you can always add the following items to your agenda:

- **Fundraising Events and Activities**
  - Brainstorm potential fundraising events or activities
  - Discuss upcoming events and assign roles or responsibilities
- **Communication Strategies**
  - Request feedback on existing communication methods (emails, social media, newsletters)
  - Discuss strategies for improving outreach and engagement

Enlisting a team has been a game-changer for our Fully Funded Academy members, lightening their load and speeding up their support raising. Remember, you're not meant to do this alone. Ministry is a team effort.

For some, the journey of support-raising is just beginning, while others have been on this path for a while. Perhaps you've had success in the past, but you feel as if you're bumping up against some invisible ceiling. We can say this from experience: Oftentimes, this comes down to shifting the people you surround yourself with. If you reflect on your past successes and breakthroughs, they probably came through another person. We can get so focused on "what" and the "how" that we lose sight of "who" can help us. The right "who" often knows the "what" and the "how."

Advancing to the next level almost always means surrounding yourself with new people. If you've been feeling stuck, it could be because you're in the same circle. You may have a board or advisory group that hasn't changed in years. They're probably wonderful folks, but if you're always with the same group, you'll likely repeat the same patterns.

I've been part of many teams and boards, and I've seen how people can become complacent. That's why I emphasize building teams with individuals who will push you and have the skills to elevate you.

Fundraising is always evolving. What worked in the past might not work now, especially with new technologies and changing behaviors. The strategies that brought you here won't necessarily take you further.

One thing that remains the same: People still want to support good causes. You're not out of options. Remember, effective fundraising is not a solo sport. If you take action, we're confident you'll see greater results!

✷✷✷

Here's a list of action items based on what we've covered in this chapter:

1. Create your Team Document.
2. Enlist your team leader.
3. Enlist other team members.
4. Schedule your first team meeting.
5. Host your first team meeting.

Be sure to take advantage of the scripts we've provided so you can save time. If you haven't done so already, they're all in the free workbook at FullyFundedAcademy.com. It contains the Team Document template, meeting agenda template, and more. Remember: cast vision, remove friction, and build bridges!

CHAPTER 4

Enhance Your Brand

"Did you hear? Pastor Eric is visiting to preach at the weekend services; it's going to be amazing. You should definitely come!"

"Who's leading worship next Sunday? If it's Sarah, I'll go, but if it's that other guy, then I'm not going. I just don't like his style."

"The senior pastor isn't preaching this Sunday? Then we should ditch church this weekend; it's not like we'll miss much anyway."

We've all heard (or made) these kinds of comments more often than we might like to admit. We gather to worship God, yet we often make decisions based on our preferences about preachers, music, and more. Like it or not, people do the same when deciding who to support.

These preferences are based on an expectation of quality and reputation from these preachers, worship leaders, churches, and more. Their "brand" plays a significant role in how people perceive and respond to them. Branding, whether we like it or not, plays a pivotal role in how ministries and leaders are perceived, especially when it comes to raising money.

Everything I Learned about Branding
I Learned in Youth Group

When I (Mike) was seventeen, I wrote my first worship song. At the time, I was leading worship for our small New Jersey youth group and absolutely loved being involved in ministry. While other kids were buying comic books and video games, I spent any money I had on worship CDs. My favorites were from Vineyard Music, and I'd often spend hours poring over their *Touching the Father's Heart* or *Winds of Worship* albums, trying out songs that could work well at church.

It wasn't long before I realized the simple fact that some songs were better than others, that some worship leaders had built a reputation for writing popular songs, and that those worship leaders were featured more often on albums. (If you must know, my favorites were David Ruis and Brian Doerksen.)

When I taught my song to our band during rehearsal, they liked it! They asked where they could get a recording of it, and oddly enough, I lied! I just said it was just some old Vineyard song that there was no recording of because I actually thought it would sound prideful to tell them I wrote a song. It's a bit ridiculous now that I think of it, but that's how averse I was to taking credit for anything.

Eventually, word got out that I wrote that song, and I ended up writing many more. Several of them got traction, and I started getting invitations to lead worship at other churches and even conferences. I always dreamed of having one of my songs on a Vineyard album. I wasn't aware at the time that those recordings were only from worship leaders at Vineyard churches, and since I didn't attend one, the chances were almost nil.

While my songs were well-received, I always wondered if there was something more that needed to be done to get them out there. Clearly, multiple congregations were using them, and I thought getting them on a recording would help more churches. A friend once told me, "Man, if people thought one of those Vineyard worship leaders wrote your song and it was on an album, everyone would use it. It's just as good as the others, but no one knows you."

That was the first time I realized that branding is a very real phenomenon, even (or especially) in ministry.

What Is Branding and Is It Really Necessary?

"Branding" stems from the old ranching practice of burning an identifying mark onto livestock with an iron. The concept of branding later expanded into business to identify products manufactured by a particular company under a particular name.

Josiah Wedgwood, an English potter born in the 1700s and often called the father of modern marketing, was perhaps the first person who leveraged branding to create a retail empire. After winning a competition hosted by Queen Charlotte, Wedgwood dubbed his pottery "Queen's Ware," opened an exclusive showroom in London for a more affluent market, and pioneered sales practices of "money-back guarantees" and "free delivery." Whether it has to do with livestock, pottery, or how we present ourselves, branding is simply about identity.

Personal branding expands branding to include a person's ideas, expertise, reputation, and personality. We intentionally craft a public identity for an express purpose. You may not speak on huge stages or lead a globally recognized ministry, but as a fundraiser who meets with potential donors face-to-face, you absolutely have a public identity. You have a *personal* brand.

Much of the personal brand space plays out in two ways. The first group of people sells a false version of themselves, thinking that image or perception alone will get them the results they seek. We've all seen examples of people "flexing" online about their lifestyle, accomplishments, and recognition on social media, and unfortunately, the ministry space is no different.

The flip side of presenting a false version of yourself is oversharing in the name of authenticity. These folks talk nonstop about their issues, sometimes revealing way more than what is even comfortable to read about. It's as if these people are trying to sell their struggles rather than provide solutions. Like a car wreck, these folks garner attention, but it's short-lived.

So, what are we to do? Here's a simple question that can serve as a litmus test for you: "Can I build a campfire around what I'm sharing?" By this, I mean, is there warmth? Are you building something that is attractive and inviting to others? Can you build a community around it? Is what you're sharing a light in the darkness?

The reality is that you and I already have a brand. We occupy an identity that varies depending on whom we talk to. Have you ever felt there is a difference between who you are at work versus who you are at home or with your best friends? If so, it's because you have a particular identity among those different groups of people. Your friends know you in a way your colleagues will never know. Those same friends may have very little knowledge of who you are at work. Yet who you are at work versus who you are at home is still you.

We want to level with you right off the bat. *Don't build your brand; become your brand.* Do the hard work required to become the person you're trying to sell to people. Embrace integrity. There is no shortcut. All this talk of becoming a better person may seem like it's coming out of nowhere, but I assure you that you won't be on this journey very long before you have to confront your own dissonance if you want to go any further.

People Want to Support Winning Causes

People naturally gravitate toward success, and they want to contribute to winning causes. Mary and I are both passionate baseball fans—she's a St. Louis fan and I'm a New York guy. You don't have to follow sports to know that the St. Louis Cardinals and New York Yankees aren't just teams; they're winning brands. Both franchises carry a legacy of excellence. Their fans expect a certain level of performance. I can't count how many players have come to New York and said in their press conferences, "There's something special about donning the Yankee pinstripes. People expect us to win, and that's what I've come here to do." It's as if these players take their commitment to play to another level when they join teams like the Yankees, Cardinals, or any other historically winning franchise. We want you to do more than simply project that air of excellence; we want you to embody it.

Years ago, a ministry colleague I'll call Terrell invited me to dinner. He was raising support for a long-term mission commitment in Asia. Despite not knowing him well, his reputation preceded him: Terrell was highly respected, was the son of a respected pastor, was well-educated, articulate, and a winner in every sense.

My willingness to support him was based on who he was—in a sense, his personal brand. The specifics of his work seemed secondary. He could have been going to Mars for all I cared; I was in.

But let's say a year or two goes by and updates from Terrell dwindle. The only time I hear from him is when he needs money. Suddenly, what he does becomes as important. I'm wondering if my support is being stewarded wisely. I start to question his reputation, competence, and ability. I wonder if there are better places to send my support. This might be hard to hear, but your donors think like this.

The 7-Step Donor Progression

If branding is about establishing an identity, then marketing is about sharing that identity with the world. Early in my career, I came across a speaker and blogger named Guy Kawasaki. At the time, his title was "Chief Evangelist" for Apple. I was a bit taken aback, thinking the term "evangelist" should be reserved for those in ministry. Apple hijacked the term and gave him that title because Kawasaki's job was to spread their "gospel."

It's natural for us to want to get word out about what God is doing in our midst, but we're often unsure of how to do it. Let's use this 7-step progression to illustrate the journey that a potential donor needs to take in order to finally get to a place of lending you their support:

7 Step Donor Progression

Know → Like → Trust → Try → Give → Repeat → Refer

First, people need to *know* about you and your mission. Without awareness, there's no foundation for a relationship. Once they know about you, the door opens to the possibility of *liking* you. This is based on the alignment of values and the appeal of your mission. But liking isn't enough; *trust* is the cornerstone. Trust is built over time through consistent, honest communication and by living out the values you profess.

Then comes the *try* phase. This is where potential supporters go for a "test drive," perhaps by reading your newsletter, checking out your social media, or hearing you preach at church. If they like what they see, they move to the *give* phase.

But your work doesn't stop there. Nurturing these relationships can lead donors to give *repeatedly*, and eventually, they become your advocates, *referring* others to your mission. Let's break this down a bit further using our missionary friends Kim and James Boley as an example:

1. **Know:** Kim and James first aim to make potential donors aware of their mission and work. They do this through social media, weekly email newsletters, and personal interactions.

2. **Like:** Once people are aware of their ministry, Kim and James focus on building a connection and rapport with potential donors. They share stories, testimonials, and personal experiences to help donors relate to their mission, and hopefully, a few people grow to like them!

3. **Trust:** In meetings and when they present in a church, they share their background, qualifications, and the impact of their work to establish credibility.

4. **Try:** Kim and James offer opportunities to "try out" their ministry by inviting potential donors to read their newsletters, volunteer at events, or participate in other small ways before asking them to financially support them on a regular, ongoing basis.

5. **Give:** Once donors have experienced their ministry and trust has been established, Kim and James invite people to give financially. They make sure they've cast a clear vision and communicated what's at stake.

6. **Repeat:** Kim and James nurture their relationships with donors to encourage ongoing support. They give regular updates, express gratitude, and show the impact of donations to encourage donors to continue giving.

7. **Refer:** Finally, Kim and James encourage donors to refer others to their ministry. They ask their current donors to make introductions to new friends and create opportunities for their current donors to share their positive experiences with others.

Unfortunately, many missionaries start immediately at the *give* phase, unaware that it's their responsibility to build out the essential steps of *Know, Like, Trust,* and *Try.* To do this, we need to communicate clearly and turn all the work we've done so far into what we call the Three Sticky Stories.

The Three Sticky Stories

These three stories are going to be the foundation of your fundraising communication:

1. **The Founder's Story:** This is your "origin" story and how you came to have a heart for missions or ministry.

2. **The Organization's Story:** This is about the birth of your calling, ministry, or the start of your involvement with a particular organization.

3. **The Transformation Story:** This story is about the transformation experienced by those you minister to.

Missionaries often prioritize the Transformation Story with its testimonials and case studies. However, the Founder's Story and the Organization's Story are just as important.

You might feel you're in over your head when it comes to storytelling, but if you answered the questions we asked in chapter 1, "What pisses you off, what breaks your heart, and what is the big problem you solve?" then you have the foundations to the Founder's Story and Organization's Story. For your Founder's Story, simply share the answers to what pisses you off and what breaks your heart. One of the questions we're often asked is, "What if we can't disclose the work or ministry we do because we're in closed nations or the work we do can't be publicized?" This is why having *all* of these stories is so important. Let's look at an example.

Founder's and Organization's Story: Love146

One of the nonprofits I've supported over the years is Love146 (Love146.org), dedicated to providing survivor care for children rescued out of the sex trade.

For very obvious reasons, they can't plaster their marketing materials with the faces of the kids they've helped. So, Love146 relies heavily on the story of its founder, Rob Morris. He is active in using social media platforms and initially got the word out by speaking at churches and youth conferences to share how he came into this work and how Love146 was born.

I'm going to quote Rob quite a bit in the next few sections because I want you to see how powerful it can be to have these stories in your fundraising arsenal. These quotes are taken from an interview with Rob on one of my podcasts, which you can listen to at MikeKim.com/yatb293. (Note: I've paraphrased his answers to be more suitable for reading rather than a direct word-for-word transcript.) When asked about how he got into this line of work, this is what Rob said:

***

"My wife and I have always had a heart, specifically for vulnerable children. It's how we have built our family through the years, through adoption. Years ago, back in 2001 or 2002, some friends and I started hearing about this thing called child trafficking. We were just like, 'What is this? And why is this? I can't believe that this is happening in the world.' Back in 2002, not a lot of people knew what human trafficking was; the terminology was just recently coined to describe this kind of crime against children.

"We started researching and educating ourselves. We all had different public platforms. I had been doing some public speaking before that and was actually a drummer in a band during that time. This other friend of mine was the lead singer of another band. We had an artist, a photographer. We had public platforms and thought, 'Maybe we could use these public platforms to raise awareness about this, maybe raise some funds for organizations doing something about it.'

"In that process, we connected with another organization that was basically made up of criminal investigators and lawyers who work in this field. One of my friends became good friends with the CEO of an organization who said, 'Look, if you guys are gonna be talking about this publicly, you should really understand it because it's pretty complex.' He invited us to one of their operating centers to see firsthand."

(Note: Rob now flows naturally into the story of his organization, Love 146. Remember, for your Organization Story, simply share your answers to the question, "What is the big problem you're trying to solve?" Now, back to Rob.)

"We traveled to a southeast Asian country and connected with their team there on the ground. They happened to be in the middle of an investigation of a brothel where it was suspected that children were being sold and trafficked. They were going in on this particular night and said, 'Do you want to come in with us?' We would never recommend an organization do this. Leave it to the professional investigators. But because of the relationship we had with them, they trusted us.

"What they do is go undercover, posing as customers wearing undercover surveillance equipment, and gather evidence to do a separate investigation of local law enforcement. There's a lot of corruption involved. A lot of times, these law enforcement people are being paid by brothel managers or traffickers to look the other way or even for protection. To this day, it was probably one of the most disturbing experiences of my life--to pretend to be the very thing that everything in me is completely and utterly repulsed by.

"I remember one of the last things they said before we went into this brothel, 'If you don't think you can hold it together, don't come in because we can't risk you freaking out with what you're about to see, breaking character, and destroying this investigation.'

"We said, 'No worries'--until we walked into this place. We found ourselves standing in a room looking through these glass windows. Young girls were sitting in rows wearing matching red dresses, having even the dignity of a name stripped from them. They just had numbers pinned to their dresses.

"On this side of the glass, I'm standing shoulder to shoulder with predators who were purchasing these kids for sex. The brothel workers were walking around with menus with the numbers of the children, their specialty of what they can do, and all of that.

"I remembered at that moment the words of that investigator, 'If you don't think you can hold it together . . .' because everything in me as a man, as a father, as a human being was not holding it together. I'm thinking, 'I want to smash through this glass right now and try to get as many of these kids out of here. How many of these guys in this room could we take out?'

"The thing that so took my breath away was the looks in the eyes of these kids. Having seven kids of my own, one of the few things I've learned about children is that if there should be anybody on the planet who has a spark in their eye, it should be a child. Looking through that glass, that was missing. Trauma does horrific things to a human being. Yet, at the same time, the body has an amazing ability to shut down when things get too traumatic and crazy. These kids were sitting there watching children's cartoons on crackling little television sets and just had these blank stares on their faces. I don't know what was happening in their heads, but it was a horrific thing to witness.

"They all were in that place except for one girl. She was the only one not looking at the television set. She was staring in our direction through the glass and the look in her eyes was different. I don't know whether it was fight in her eyes or trauma that created that look, but that stare--I'll never forget it. I will never forget her eyes, her face, or her number. Her number was 146.

"When we named the organization, it was to remember that this isn't just about issues and causes. It was about real human beings. Coming back home and wrestling through what we could do about this, eventually, through educating ourselves and learning as much as we could, we started an organization. We didn't want to reinvent any wheels. We're not criminal investigators, but we saw missing pieces that could be helpful.

"We eventually started what became Love146. We've been working for the last nineteen years on four continents through our survivor care programs and prevention programs. We've reached a little over 65,000 kids in the nineteen years we've been doing this work."

✱✱✱

This story hits me hard every time. About a year after meeting Rob, I was privileged to travel on a partner trip to see their operations and meet some of the kids they helped. It was a swell of emotions, and I don't think I've ever cried so much in my life. I've been a supporter of Love146 ever since, and it's probably not hard to see why. I was so impressed by their strategy, heart, logistics, research, and their history--they've been doing this work for over twenty years. While it would be a disservice to call Rob a fundraiser or marketer, he uses those principles to raise funds for the organization and, ultimately, help these children.

A Transformation Story

When it comes to the Transformation Story, your goal is to share the before and after of what a person or community has experienced. Let's gently shift our focus to the nuts and bolts structural elements that make a transformation story so powerful. Then, we'll circle back to one more story from Rob.

1. **Start with the Background:** Set the scene by describing the circumstances or challenges faced. This might include the specific conditions of the community, individual struggles, or broader issues that your mission seeks to address.

2. **Introduce the Character(s):** Every good story has a central character. In a Transformation Story, this could be an individual, a family, or a community your mission has impacted.

3. **Highlight the Change:** Illustrate the transformation clearly. What interventions or actions did your mission take? How did the character interact with these efforts? What are the tangible results and improvements? Use vivid descriptions, and, if possible, incorporate direct quotes or testimonies from those affected.

4. **Use Emotional Appeal:** Share heartfelt moments, struggles, and triumphs. Let your audience feel the hope, desperation, joy, and gratitude that are part of the journey.

5. **Include Visual Elements:** If possible, use before-and-after photos or videos to visually represent the transformation. Visuals can be incredibly powerful in conveying the impact of your work.

6. **Connect to the Bigger Picture:** Tie the individual story back to the larger mission of your organization. How does this story reflect the broader goals and values of your work? This helps the audience see the story as part of a larger narrative.

7. **Respect Privacy and Dignity:** Always prioritize the dignity and privacy of those in your stories. Obtain consent to share their stories and images, and be sensitive to how they are portrayed.

If you overlay all these elements together, you'll see that Rob's stories are full of these seven elements. Let's look at one more story from Rob. As you read it, consider how he weaves these seven elements into his narrative.

✱✱✱

"There was a band called Paramore that used to support our work in a really generous way. They did a concert in Manila years ago and invited the children from our safe homes in that area to come as VIP guests. All the kids knew who Paramore was, and they couldn't believe they were going to see a Paramore concert. They were so stoked that all you heard in our safe homes for weeks were Paramore songs blaring. It was an outdoor concert, and Paramore canceled their normal meet-and-greets with their fan clubs so they could specifically hang out with our kids.

"When the concert started, they all had patches with the number 146 representing not just the organization but also the girl who basically was the inspiration for our organization. They had 146 on their guitar straps and the kick drum on the drum kit, and Haley, the lead singer, wore a 146 patch.

"Our kids are in the front row screaming and just being teenage kids for a night. At one point, Haley says, 'This next song is like the first love song we've written. And I want to dedicate it tonight to some special friends of mine who are here, the children of Love146.'

"Our kids just started freaking out and started to chant '146! 146!' and it spread through the crowd. All I could think the rest of the night was, 'If only that girl who once wore that number could see this now. These children are taking their lives back, in recovery, and are on that hard journey hearing that number being chanted.'

"We have this term at Love 146: *defiant hope*. People sometimes say, 'You're such an optimistic person.' I am not an optimist by any stretch of the imagination. I admire optimists. I've seen too much to be an optimist, but I am hopeful. We've attached defiance to hope because, growing up, the word 'defiant' was always a negative thing. That defiance, now attached to hope, is paying off in spades. I think it's an act of defiance that, in the face of despair, to be hopeful is pushing back against that, insisting that change can happen."

✳✳✳

As of this writing, Love146 has reached over 81,000 children through its prevention education and survivor care efforts worldwide. They have facilitators in thirty-two states for their prevention education curriculum, "Not a Number." Their effectiveness is measured through three independent, rigorous evaluations, two of which are supported by the CDC and the Department of Justice.

Some of their children have been willing to share powerful testimonials (their faces are hidden for obvious reasons) such as, "Love146 helps kids like me get right back on track," "Now I have the words to explain how I was taken advantage of," "You showed me that I'm not defined by my past, you helped me find who I am," and "Love146 taught me that I am not disgusting."

When all of these elements come together, you can see just how powerful and effective their narrative can be.

The Three Identities of Your Brand

Let's close out this chapter with some practical steps. A successful brand has three sub-identities: Visual, Verbal, and Value. These three sub-identities are like the three legs of a tripod; even a slight imbalance can cause the whole structure to topple.

1. **Visual Identity:** The logo, pictures, fonts, color schemes, and layout of your marketing assets.
2. **Verbal Identity:** The written voice of the brand, including its choice of words, style, tone, and reading level.
3. **Value Identity:** The perceived value of the brand and how they are positioned compared to others. If you think of some brands or businesses you're familiar with, they can range from high-end (luxury) to more accessible (budget-friendly).

Eventually, you want all three of these to align with one another. If you have a great-looking website but your writing is sloppy and full of typos and poor grammar, your value identity will be tarnished. If you write well but your newsletters or social posts look like clipart from Microsoft Word in 1996, it won't resonate well, especially in today's online world. If you walk into a high-end luxury store like Louis Vuitton, you'll never hear them use words like "sale" or "discount" like they often do at Walmart.

All that to say, you don't need professional marketing materials to raise money well. What matters is simply awareness and intention. Here are a few practical tips:

- **Don't overlook email.** In the world of digital communication, it's easy to fall into the trap of trying to be everywhere at once, especially on social media. Email stands out for several reasons. First, it provides a private, direct line of communication with your supporters. Unlike social media, where algorithm changes can bury your content, an email lands right in the recipient's inbox. Your message is more likely to be seen and read.
  Also, email doesn't demand the constant upkeep of visual content like Instagram or YouTube. You don't need to worry about the perfect photo or spend hours editing a video. An email can be as simple or as detailed as you like, but it always remains a straightforward, text-based medium that values substance over style.

  Building an email list is a valuable asset for any brand. Your readers are on your list because they've chosen to hear from you, so talk to them! We recommend sending an email once a week and a bare minimum of once a month. Your email list will be one of your most reliable channels for raising support. Better yet, you actually own your email list. Unlike social media channels that can deplatform you, your email list is yours.

  A quick note here: Break up text into shorter paragraphs. Most people will read your emails and newsletters on their phones, which means long paragraphs will overwhelm them. As a general rule, I write no more than three sentences per paragraph for emails and newsletters. You may be a wordier writer, but it's necessary to get into the habit of saying more with less.

- **Your headshot is your best logo.** Use the same headshot over all your social media accounts if you have any. They say a picture is worth a thousand words, so use that to your advantage. One note: Many missionaries raise personal support for their families, so they wonder if their profile pictures or social media accounts should be "joint" accounts with their spouse or kids. We'll leave that to you, but for the most part, I advise keeping them separate.

  Typically, one person becomes the "face" of the ministry anyway, and it's much easier to have the updates or posts come from that person, who then, in turn, mentions the rest of the family. Also, if you post profile pictures of you and your spouse or your entire family, it's hard to see because the pictures are so small on social media apps. Remember, you want clarity. The rule of thumb with logos: If it looks good small, it will look good big. When you post a family photo, it may look good when blown up to size, but when shrunk down on Facebook, Instagram, or any other app, it's difficult to make out who is even in it.

- **Slogans are overrated, so don't waste too much time on them.** We mentioned back in the first chapter that you don't need a slogan; you need clarity. When it comes to branding, nothing stands alone—meaning that even a slogan needs context for it to be effective. Consider a catchy slogan like "Bridging the gap between where you are and where you want to be." Without context, it's open to interpretation. You could easily think this slogan is for a travel agency, life coach, or financial advisor. The slogan itself has very little meaning. But if you were to see it on the website of a travel agency, life coach, or financial advisor, it would make sense because there is *context*. Spend more time on building context in your fundraising efforts by writing engaging emails, effective support letters (which we'll cover in a later chapter), and good stories, like we've covered in this chapter.

Branding and Marketing Do Not Diminish Your Faith in God

So, is all this branding and marketing stuff really necessary? We believe it is. While He was fully God, Jesus didn't paint a message across the sky. He utilized human principles to communicate and spread the greatest message of all. His disciples were diverse, including fishermen, doctors, and lawyers, effectively reaching all strata of society. Many of these disciples were bilingual, particularly the fishermen, who traveled extensively and spread news of his works far and wide.

Jesus based much of his work out of Capernaum, a bustling trade city by the water frequented by many travelers, which facilitated the spread of his message. He often taught using stories, universally recognized as one of the most effective ways to engage and be remembered by human beings.

It's crucial to recognize that marketing your efforts doesn't diminish your faith in God's plans. There's a saying I often use in training sessions: "Marketing isn't about closing a sale; it's about opening a relationship." Open up new relationships, that's all we want you to do.

Friend, let's get over our aversion to marketing. Failing to promote your ministry is doing a disservice to the very people you've been called to serve. On that note, we leave you with one of the most famous quotes of modern times, most often attributed to political historian Edmund Burke: "The only thing necessary for the triumph of evil is for good men to do nothing." No, it's not Scripture, but it's true. What is also true is that you are doing important things to serve people, and that is nothing to be bashful about.

✱✱✱

We covered a lot in this chapter, and we'll cover even more in the next one. For now, take a breath and let the insights sink in.

Looking at the 7-Step Donor Progression, what resonated most with you? Are there aspects of their method you might have overlooked or underestimated in your own fundraising efforts? Consider where you might enhance your approach to deepen trust and engagement with potential and existing supporters.

1. Reading through the story of Love146, what did you notice about how Rob's stories made you feel? Can you see why they have such a compelling narrative?
2. Using all of these examples as context, start jotting down a rough draft of your Three Sticky Stories, using your answers from chapter 1.
3. Review the last five or so emails you've sent to your list and evaluate them based on what you've learned. Where is there room for improvement? Can you break up the text a little more? Have you been emailing your list enough?
4. Change your profile pictures across your social media accounts to use the same headshot.

Remember, we've put these exercises in a convenient downloadable workbook, which you can download for free at FullyFundedAcademy.com.

CHAPTER 5

Deploy Your Team

Whew! We've covered a lot so far, so let's take a bit of a breather and set some reasonable expectations on getting all the things done. The work outlined so far will require quite a bit of writing, particularly around the stories we covered in the last chapter. There's still other work to do, but as we mentioned back in chapter 1, all of this work *prepares you for your moment*. Once this work is done, you'll have a strategic and intentional foundation to work from and be ready for any opportunities that may come along. As the old saying goes, "The opportunity of a lifetime needs to be seized during the lifetime of the opportunity."

In this chapter, we'll talk about deploying your team. In essence, this means equipping your team with the resources they need in order to do what they've committed to do. There's a good reason to leverage your team: In some contexts, they're often going to be more effective and persuasive than you. The fact that your team isn't you often makes them a stronger, more credible voice for your ministry.

While I (Mary) was leading fundraising efforts for a well-known organization, one of our volunteers I'll call Kathy introduced me to a businessman I'll call Don.

Don was interested in supporting us, and since he was Kathy's connection, we went together to meet Don at his office. Imagine my surprise when Don asked Kathy (not me), "Why did *you* take the time to be here? You have a family and you don't get paid for this, right?"

Kathy told Don that she was indeed an unpaid volunteer. She shared her story about the impact our organization had on her and her loved ones and how she didn't want others in similar situations to be without help. Don was taken by Kathy's response. Being a businessman, Don believed very strongly that time meant money, and he was impressed that Kathy would take time out of her busy schedule to volunteer. Kathy and I left the meeting with a signed commitment of support from Don.

That meeting was a turning point in how I fundraised. I had been trained on the importance of the staff and volunteer partnership for years, but this meeting allowed me to see it firsthand. Don didn't want to hear from a paid staff member telling him why his money was going to make a difference. He wanted to hear from a volunteer who could tell him why he should care.

We've all had the experience of telling our friends about a restaurant or product we really like, or vice versa. Word-of-mouth marketing is one of the best forms of marketing out there. No one paid your friend to tell you about a great restaurant--they just couldn't help but tell you because they loved their experience there. This is a far cry from the owner of the restaurant telling you why you should come in.

We want this to be a really simple and actionable chapter because it shouldn't take too much to give your team what they need to make things smoother for them. In short, you need to provide them with three things:

1. One-Pager (Case Document)
2. Title
3. Conversation Starters

There's a saying: "You never get a second chance to make a first impression." That is not only true of you, but it will be true of your team members. Give them every opportunity to successfully convey the importance of your mission. Now, let's dig further into each of these.

Your One-Pager

In the fundraising world, a case document is a concise, compelling overview of your ministry's work, designed to help potential supporters understand your mission and feel inspired to donate. Essentially, it's a "case for support." It serves as your sales piece, providing a snapshot of your background, mission, and funding needs.

Please Note: This document should not be mass-mailed to potential donors. This is a "sales" document and should be used for your fundraising meetings when you are making the ask.

The document is crafted to quickly and clearly communicate your story and encourage potential supporters to take action. Typically, this document includes a brief bio, an overview of your ministry, and a call to action for support. A well-crafted One-Pager is a powerful tool for several reasons:

1. **Clarity and Conciseness:** The document provides a clear and concise overview of your work, making it easier for supporters to understand and connect with your mission.
2. **Inspiration:** A compelling case document can inspire potential supporters by highlighting the impact of your work and the difference they can make by donating to your mission.
3. **Professionalism:** A well-designed case document conveys professionalism and can help you make a positive impression on potential supporters.
4. **Efficiency:** The document can be easily shared with potential supporters, allowing you to reach more people more efficiently.

If you are raising less than, say, $100,000 in one single campaign, you don't need to overwhelm a potential donor with anything more than a one-sided sheet of paper. If you are raising over $100,000, we recommend expanding this document (some of our students go up to eight pages). If a donor is being asked to consider giving to a ministry that is raising over six figures, they'll probably need more details about your ministry to feel confident giving a much larger gift.

Regardless, here's how to best use your One-Pager in a meeting:

- Start by introducing yourself and your mission. Use the document to provide a brief overview of your background and the work you do.
- Use the middle section of the document to provide an overview of your ministry and the impact you are making. Highlight key goals and achievements to date.
- Use the bottom section of the document to make a clear and compelling call to action. Invite potential supporters to donate and provide easy ways for them to do so.

You can see how your One-Pager can serve as a conversation starter. Be prepared to answer questions and provide more detail about your mission as questions arise.

Create Your One-Pager, Step-by-Step

We'll provide a template for you to work from in the following section, but for now, let's look at the steps you need to take to put all of this together. You'll see how your answers to the exercises from the previous chapters will now come into play.

1. **Gather Information.** Before you start creating your case document, gather all the necessary information. This includes your personal background, mission statement, ministry goals, and funding needs.
2. **Write Your Bio.** Write a brief bio that highlights your background, mission, and passion for your work. Pull from your answers to the questions from chapters 1 and 4 and weave them into the script in the template below. This section will allow you to connect with potential supporters on a personal level.
3. **Describe Your Ministry.** Describe your ministry and the impact you are making. Pull from your answers to the question, "What is the big problem you're trying to solve?" Highlight your mission and vision, as well as any specific goals you are working toward.

4. **Call to Action.** In the bottom third of the document, you will post a clear call to action. Invite potential supporters to donate and provide information on how they can do so.

5. **Design and Layout.** Design your document to be visually appealing and easy to read. We've provided a basic template to follow, but you will want to infuse your design with images, colors, and fonts that reflect your mission and style. The primary image at the top of the page should be a professional headshot of you, you and your spouse, or you and your family. Any other images, should you choose to use them, should be a prompt to the stories you like to tell when making your ask.

6. **Review and Edit.** Before finalizing your document, review it carefully for errors and ensure that it effectively communicates your message. Be sure the team you enlisted in chapter 3 reviews it and gives you their feedback.

7. **Print Copies.** Once your document is complete, print out a handful of copies to have with you at all times. You never want to be caught off guard. Also, have a digital version available to email as a follow-up to an impromptu meeting. Your One-Pager should be given to your team so they can use it when making direct appeals. Again, a reminder: Your One-Pager should not be sent en masse to potential donors. This should be used in meetings when an ask is made.

✷✷✷

One-Pager Template

[Top Section]

- Name:
- Title (if applicable):
- Sending organization (if applicable):
- Headshot of Individual or Family:

- Personal logo or sending organization logo:

[About You: approximately 50 words]

Born and raised in _____ (location if relevant), _____ (missionary) serves as _____ (title) _____ (what do you do).

(In this section, highlight the injustice you see and the compassion you carry—what pisses you off and what breaks your heart. These are the exercises you went through in chapter 1. If you want to quote yourself here or incorporate a testimonial from another leader or someone you've helped, you can feature that as well. Just be sure to keep this short.)

[About the Ministry + clear and compelling goal: approximately 50–75 words]

Here's the vision we have for _____. (You can expound more after this opening line.)

Our goal is to ____ (do) _____ (#) ____ (people) by ____ (date)——and we can't do it alone.

Will you join us?

[Call to Action Section]

Yes, I/we want to support _____.

Please accept our gift of $____ per month/year (suggested gift of $100/month).

Yes, I/we want to support the ____ (special project)

Please accept our gift of $____ to purchase _____.

[Donor's info:]

Name:

Address:

Phone:

Email:

To make an online donation, go to: [info]

Mail donations to: [info]

***

Real Example of a One-Pager

Take a look at the One-Pager by one of our members, Emily Houser. We looked at Emily's Team Document in chapter 3, and now we'll look at her One-Pager. She has kindly granted us permission to share it, and you can download it as part of our free workbook at FullyFundedAcademy.com.

EMILY HOUSER

**Correctional Chaplain, President of
Smoky Mountain Dream Center**

Born and raised in Appalachia, Emily Houser serves as a U.S. Missionary and Correctional Chaplain sharing the gospel with the people of Appalachia who have become victims of poverty, abuse, and incarceration. As a Correctional Chaplain, Emily knew that these women had heard about Jesus, but they didn't know Him. Many of these women are waking up with only one thing in mind, to find drugs by any means necessary. When Emily began her work in Cocke County Jail five years ago, nearly 90% of the areas offenders were finding themselves back in jail and women parolees had no access to transitional homes in the 35 counties of E. Tennessee.

Emily shares, "It is our job as ambassadors of Jesus Christ to go in there and tell them there is hope and that they can have a different life. They can have something so much better, so much more powerful, and they can leave a legacy that is so much better than what they were given."

SMOKY MOUNTAIN
Dream Center

BE A PART OF THE DREAM!
Emily and the Smoky Mountain Dream Center team are working across five states in the Appalachian region to teach Bible and Life Skills in correctional facilities, provide leadership training, literacy programs, and physical education programs in the school systems, provide food and temporary housing for women coming out of incarceration, build out a network of support among area pastors, aid in disaster relief, and work to beautify the community through construction and community projects. But the BIG dream is just coming to life as we launch the Smoky Mountain Dream Center "Building The Dream Campaign" to **purchase 100 acres of land in 100 days** (phase 1), **build the FireFly Children's Ranch** (phase 2), and **build the Smoky Mountain Dream Center** (phase 3). The Dream Center cannot function without people just like you and we invite you to help make the dream a reality!

○ Yes, I/we want to support U.S. Missionary, Emily Houser.
Please accept our gift of $_____ per month/year (suggested gift of $100/month).

○ Yes, I/we want to support the 100 Acres in 100 Days Building The Dream Campaign.
Please accept our gift of $_____ to purchase _____ acre(s) of land ($5,000/acre).

Name_____ Phone_____
Address_____ City_____ State____ Zip____
Email_____

To make an online donation go to:
giving.ag.org and type in Emily Houser #2838167
or go to **smokymountaindreamcenter.org**

Mail Donations to:
Smoky Mountain Dream Center, Attn: Emily Houser
P.O. Box 2352, Greeneville, TN 37743

Note how Emily weaves the copy (words) in with the photos. She has a nice, clear headshot of herself, and the other two photos communicate the team dynamic and an emphasis on prayer.

Titles Can Be a Key Factor in Volunteer Engagement

This may sound counter-intuitive, especially if you don't think your ministry is large enough to warrant it, but there is power in giving titles to your team members. Titles carry weight and significance. This is especially true in the context of raising money because it conveys the responsibility involved.

A volunteer introduced as the "Event Chairperson" or "Board President" immediately garners a level of seriousness and professionalism. This respect and authority are not just perceived externally but can also influence how volunteers view their roles and responsibilities. It signals that their contribution is valued and pivotal to the organization's success.

Recall how we gave a title to the team in chapter 3, even if it was to simply fundraise for personal support. We called it the Johnson Advisory Team.

> The Johnson Advisory Team is comprised of individuals, ministry, and community leaders who believe in the mission of John and Sue Johnson. The vision of the Johnson Advisory Team is not to serve as a governing board but rather to promote and support the success of the Johnsons' work through Hope Ministries in Munich, Germany. In doing so, this group will be assisting John and Sue's mission to bring the gospel to the unreached through 100 home churches throughout Germany, France, and Spain by December 31, 20xx.

You can take the same concept of titles and apply them to individual team members. Here are some possible titles that could be used or tweaked for your own situation:

1. **Support Coordination Leader:** This title is suitable for a volunteer who takes a lead role in organizing and coordinating support-raising efforts.
2. **Partnership Director:** Ideal for someone overseeing the development of partnerships and collaborations for missionary support.
3. **Fundraising Advisor:** Suitable for a volunteer who provides strategic guidance and planning in fundraising activities.
4. **Community Engagement Coordinator:** For a volunteer who focuses on engaging the community to build awareness and support for missionaries.
5. **Outreach Campaign Manager:** This title can be given to someone who manages specific fundraising campaigns or events.
6. **Donor Relations Ambassador:** Suitable for volunteers who maintain and nurture relationships with current and potential donors.
7. **Advocacy and Awareness Leader:** For someone who leads efforts in promoting the missionary's work and generating support through advocacy.
8. **Volunteer Facilitator:** Ideal for someone who recruits and manages a network of volunteers for support-raising activities.
9. **Communications and Media Liaison:** Suitable for a volunteer handling communications, social media, and public relations to support fundraising.
10. **Global Missions Connector:** Ideal for someone who focuses on connecting the missionary work with global partners and networks.

Regardless of what titles you settle on, it should resonate with the volunteer's own sense of identity and aspiration, aligning with their skills and the role they are expected to play. It should instill a sense of pride and ownership in their work. This sense of belonging and importance can lead to volunteers going the extra mile, advocating more passionately for the cause, and taking greater initiative in their roles. A title can also make it easier for your team members to open up conversations with others about supporting your work. If a team member is "just a person" who helps you out, that's very different from someone who carries a title.

Every Volunteer Should Be a Donor

We touched on this back in chapter 3 when talking about the "Give or Get Goal," but I want to circle back here and encourage you to present an opportunity for your team members to support you financially. A study released several years ago by Fidelity Charitable Gift Fund and VolunteerMatch reported that 67 percent of Americans who volunteered say they "generally make their financial donations to the same organizations where they volunteer." The study also reported that Americans who volunteer their time and skills to nonprofit organizations also donate an average of ten times more money to charity than people who don't volunteer.

Whether you and your donors are based in the United States or elsewhere, these statistics show that your team members should be asked to give financially. You may think that volunteers who donate their time feel that is good enough and don't "need" to donate financially. We encourage you not to make those assumptions. Invite them to give the same way you would invite any other donor. Here is some verbiage to help you with the process. You might say,

"Before we start inviting others to support our ministry, we want to invite you to consider a gift. We don't want to miss the opportunity to invite you to financially support the mission."

According to the US Department of Labor, in 2023, about sixty-three million people claimed to volunteer, which means nearly 25 percent of the US population volunteered somewhere, and approximately one billion people volunteered around the globe. Most US-based volunteers were between the ages of thirty-five and fifty-four, had a higher education, and volunteered with one or two organizations. One out of every three in the US volunteered with a religious organization.

Don't lower your expectations of what your volunteers are capable of giving or doing. Don't be afraid to take the lead to ensure you have an elite group of volunteers and donors who are the best representatives for you.

Now, let's look at a few subtle but powerful shifts in verbiage that can really elevate the effectiveness of everyone involved in getting you fully funded.

"Me" to "We" and the Power of Volunteer Ownership

This first one is your responsibility. Just two years after we graduated college, my husband, Geno, and I signed the paperwork on our first home in Missouri. It was a life-changing moment! We were *homeowners*. As they handed us the keys, our humble little abode went from being just "a" house to "our" house. Just like the keys to the house, you need to hand the keys over to your volunteers and give them ownership of the cause.

As soon as you change your vocabulary and start saying "we" are in this together, your team will come up with ways to make a greater impact. Encouraging your volunteers to change their speech and inviting them to be insiders in your ministry means there is no longer a "you" and "them" mentality. This just takes a little practice, but when you hear someone use the terminology that "you" should do something, it's important to correct the statement to "You mean *we* should do something?" Your volunteers and donors will quickly get the hint that you can't do this alone. As the age-old adage goes, TEAM stands for "Together Everyone Achieves More."

Now, let's look at some engaging and effective phrases your volunteers can use to open a conversation about supporting your ministry. We encourage you to print this out and give this list to your members at your first meeting (it's all in the free download at FullyFundedAcademy. com). This will equip them to open conversations with others. You might even consider working through these conversation starters with a role play exercise during a meeting. If someone on your team has experience in sales, marketing, or even customer service, they'll be able to help you!

- **"I've got something exciting to share with you"**: This sets a positive and enthusiastic tone, indicating that what follows is something worthwhile.

- **"You need to know this person"**: Use this to introduce the missionary to a potential donor and give a reason why.
- **"There's a story I think you'll find inspiring"**: This phrase invites the potential donor into a narrative rather than a straightforward ask.
- **"Have you ever thought about making a bigger difference?"**: This question directly addresses the potential donor's desire to impact the world positively, tying it to the ministry's mission.
- **"I want to introduce you to a cause that changed my life"**: Personal testimonies are compelling. This phrase shares a personal connection to the ministry.
- **"Can I share with you a cause close to my heart?"**: This phrase is gentle and personal, indicating that what's to be discussed is something deeply valued by the volunteer.
- **"Imagine if we could . . ."**: Starting with an imaginative scenario can help potential supporters envision the impact of their contribution and feel part of something larger.
- **"You're someone who understands the value of giving back"**: This phrase appeals to the listener's charitable nature, setting a positive premise for the conversation.
- **"Let's talk about transforming lives together"**: This phrase is inclusive and emphasizes the partnership aspect of support, suggesting a joint effort in making a difference.
- **"There's an opportunity I believe you'd be interested in"**: Framing things as an opportunity rather than a request can be more engaging and less imposing.
- **"I've found a way to help [specific cause/mission] and thought of you"**: This phrase personalizes the conversation, indicating why the listener, in particular, might be interested.
- **"Have you heard about [ministry name]?"**: Starting with a question about the ministry can lead to a more detailed discussion about its work and impact.

- **"Join me in supporting a cause that matters"**: A direct invitation to join in support can be effective, especially when framed as a collective effort.
- **"Your impact could be huge"**: Highlighting the potential impact of the listener's support can be a powerful motivator.

In the spirit of Matthew 10 and Luke 10, remember that each member of your team has been chosen for a purpose, much like the disciples were chosen by Jesus. They've been called to step out into their communities, their workplaces, and their circles of influence to advocate for a cause that is much bigger than any single individual. Provide them with the tools they need, but also give them the freedom to use their unique voices and talents. The work ahead may sometimes seem daunting, but with a team, you are not alone. Make sure they know how grateful you are, and don't hold back in showing them your appreciation. With your team by your side, you are capable of making an immeasurable impact!

✳✳✳

The most important action item in this chapter is to complete your One-Pager. It's essential to have this ready as we head into the next chapter, Organize Your Ask.

1. Complete your One-Pager.
2. Consider giving titles to your team members.
3. Print out the Conversation Starters for your team members.

Remember, you can grab all the resources in a convenient workbook free at FullyFundedAcademy.com.

CHAPTER 6

Organize Your Ask

Your relationship with potential supporters can be a bit like dating and marriage. It won't always work out, and if they do, things can take time. If the relationship goes well then at some point you'll want to "pop the question." In the fall of 1999, I (Mary) entered my sophomore year of college. Only a few weeks into the semester, I met Geno, the guy who would become my husband.

The first time I saw Geno was at a weeknight Bible study in the ballroom of the university student union. He played the drums for the worship team that night, and I distinctly remember him running across the room when the service ended to jump on the back of a guy at least a foot taller than him. Geno was energetic, loud, and appeared to enjoy being the center of attention. That day, we passed by each other and remained strangers for weeks. We met that September, started dating in October, and a year later, we were engaged. Two years after that, we got married and now have a wonderful daughter.

There are many strangers to your ministry today, but one day, some of those folks could become your strongest supporters. While some people get married almost as soon as they meet, it isn't the norm. It certainly isn't the norm when it comes to your relationship with potential donors, especially when it comes to asking them to give. Remember: Know, Like, Trust, Try, Give, Repeat, Refer.

Missionaries often wonder how they can overcome the fear or discomfort of asking for support. The best place to start is to get organized. Just like Geno had to get a few things in order before he proposed (ha!), it's time for you to get things in order and prepare for your moment.

In this chapter, we want to help you organize your ask. We'll look at different sources of support, the often hidden factors behind why people donate, and some of the other elements you'll want to have in place as you get ready to make your appeal.

Let's start by looking at the kinds of sources you can reach out to for support, which often break down into these categories:

1. Family
2. Friends
3. Churches (or other ministries)
4. Individuals
5. Businesses

The most common source of support is from individuals who earn their income. It's no surprise that the fist tends to be tighter with these folks since they're giving out of their personal finances. If you have a strong relationship with individual donors, their giving can withstand the ups and downs of life, like a change in a job, a big move, having children, or a death in the family.

Individual supporters can often be family or friends, and this can be the easiest or the hardest request to make. Asking a family member or friend for support can be straightforward because of their familiarity and love for you. Yet this same closeness can make things challenging. If they're passionate about your mission, they should be on your prospect list. However, if they've never shown interest, you may want to buffer your expectations. It can be a delicate dynamic in your relationships since you risk becoming the relative or friend who's always selling something, like those who sell multi-level marketing products like Tupperware or Mary

Kay to everyone they know. Doing so isn't necessarily bad, but it can alter your relationships significantly.

I've personally had negative experiences with direct marketing from family and friends to the extent of losing friendships over it. No one enjoys feeling pressured, nor should they donate to you simply because of a personal connection. Even if they do contribute, such donors may quickly retract their support if given an opportunity. Relying on friends and family for the bulk of your support can lack sustainability.

Share naturally about your work and fundraising goals. If they express interest and want to support you, that's wonderful. However, avoid creating an expectation that they must contribute. Your calling isn't their calling. Be sensitive with this group; after all, they are the ones you cherish the most. The last thing you want is for family gatherings to feel like a fundraising event.

When it comes to churches supporting you, there are a few ways this can happen. A church can support you financially, either monthly or sometimes with an annual gift. When Mike was on staff at a church in Connecticut, they supported over twelve full-time missionaries monthly with gifts in the thousands.

In lieu of that, some churches may take a few weekends out of the year to raise money from the congregation for you or take the full offering one weekend and split it among all the missionaries they support. At Mike's church, they often had certain missionaries preach during the weekend services, collect the offering, and give a portion or all of the funds to that ministry.

If you approach the leadership at your church to request these kinds of opportunities, you need to be prepared. At a minimum, make sure you have the One-Pager we outlined in the previous chapter ready. Pastor Josh Finley, a longtime friend of Mike's, advises missionaries to look for ways to align their initiatives with the church's core values, mission, and areas of interest in that particular season. Josh has served in numerous pastoral roles, from youth pastor to campus pastor to lead pastor. He recommends that missionaries proactively engage with church leaders to understand how best to connect with their congregations rather than assuming preaching opportunities are the best approach. Josh says, "Instead of assuming what you think would be best, you should ask the pastor . . . what's the best way to engage your congregation and your people?" In other words, build the relationship.

Another example that underscores this premise can be found in a fundraising campaign Josh spearheaded while lead pastor of the church. The goal was to raise money to fund their satellite campus. This was a significant challenge because the main campus of Josh's church was in a village town and they were looking to plant a satellite campus in a nearby city. The members of his church had very different backgrounds than those they were trying to reach in the city.

Josh filled his calendar with about fifty individual meetings within a two-month period *before* he even went public about the campaign. He learned that people gave to a person (him) before they gave to the project and that life moves at the speed of relationships. In turn, relationships move at the speed of trust.

"Before I went public to ask, I needed to master the one-on-one individual conversation. The more I did it, the more confident I got. I started with the people I was going to be the most comfortable with, those who were well-resourced but also had a lot of trust with. After about ten or fifteen of those, the next thirty to forty meetings went a lot easier—even with people I didn't have as much of a relationship with. I just started to get comfortable in my own skin."

As an opener to his one-on-one conversations, Josh would start by saying something along the lines of, "I just want to thank you before I even share what's on my heart because we wouldn't be having this conversation if you hadn't already been giving, been faithful, and been a part of this vision, this church, this house. But here's the problem: We need to expand, and here's why." Consider using some form of this opening when speaking with past supporters whom you may be asking for more support from.

Josh continues, "People buy into you as a person before they buy into your project. We can't try to sell people on a product if they don't even understand all the ins and outs of the product—to do multi-site with the technology involved—especially in a village like that.So, before you ever try to sell someone on the product, sell them on the process. I imagined someone asking me, "What process have you gone through to come to this place where you even think this is a good idea?"

Then Josh would respond by outlining the process by which he came to believe in this initiative: a lot of time in prayer, bringing the idea before the church elders, hiring consultants, traveling around the country to meet with others who had done this successfully, and so forth. He wanted potential supporters to know that he did his homework.

During those one-on-one meetings, Josh would then allow folks to ask questions and he'd ask them, "Would you be willing to pray and have God lead you to the most sacrificial gift you could give toward this goal?"

Josh's experiences have been incredibly helpful to our members in Fully Funded Academy, and we hope you'll take his insights to heart and apply them to your situation. One more note on churches: On a practical level, many churches these days plan their weekend schedules and sermon topics way ahead of time, sometimes up to a year in advance. This often includes who they will have preaching in those services, so preaching opportunities may not be as available as they used to be.

***

When it comes to raising support from businesses, be aware that your values need to align. Business owners also need to be careful about what kind of organizations they can publicly support, especially if their business isn't a "Christian business" or they have to run their giving decisions by a board or other leaders.

To work around this, many Christians start nonprofits around a cause that can cast a wider net for raising money while still being founded and operated on biblical principles, such as the prevention of sex trafficking, initiatives to meet felt needs, or education. One of our good friends, James Harrington, does this with his organization, the Ugandan Water Project. I got to know James through Mike, and they knew each other from serving in worship ministry together in their twenties. While James operates his organization based on Christian principles and with Christian staff members, the organization isn't overtly Christian. As a result, they've been able to access corporate gifts and even government connections, all while staying true to their vision.

Every situation is different, but it's wise to understand the lay of the land so you can prayerfully consider and strategize what may be best for you.

What Are Gifts-In-Kind?

There are two types of donations that can be given to your organization. The first is cash, and the second is an in-kind donation of an asset, which can often be a product, resource, or a service. Whether it's someone offering their home for a meeting, a business providing airline miles for travel, or a supporter writing a check, all roads lead back to financial support one way or another. They're all different currencies of the same generous spirit.

Make a list of all the products and services you're currently paying for and see if a supporter would be interested in covering any of those expenses. In-kind donations are often an easier request to make. For example, imagine if a neighbor knocked on your door to ask for some sugar. You'd probably go right to your pantry and wouldn't think anything of it. Imagine that same neighbor knocking on your door asking if you'd give them a couple of dollars to buy sugar. Your attitude may change simply because they requested money.

In this sense, you can use in-kind donations to your advantage and eliminate expenses, so you ultimately need less cash. Look at your budget and highlight the products and services on your expense list. Are you paying for a meeting space, sound equipment, web hosting, laptops, books, or Bibles? Some of your donors may be interested in covering these costs, especially if they have a background or resources in those fields.

If you are raising a personal budget, you may ask for gifts-in-kind for things like groceries, utilities, medical expenses, travel, or a cell phone. However, we wouldn't recommend leading with asking for gifts-in-kind for personal expenses, as donors typically don't want to feel like they are paying your bills. Ultimately, donors want to be invited to be a part of your mission, so lead with that, and if the relationship with a particular supporter warrants this and you have a need for it, you can broaden that conversation.

Levels of Financial Commitment

Below are some general breakdowns that may help, and we'll loosely use the relationship analogy to guide us. These aren't hard and fast amounts, so don't get too caught up in the exact figures. Rather, consider the level of commitment and closeness of the relationship involved.

- **The First Date:** These might be gifts of $25 or less total. They might include contributions from an offering at your church or a small fundraiser like a bake sale or car wash. These donations require minimal commitment from you and the donor.
- **The Second Date:** Gifts of $50–$100 or more. These are initial gifts or donations, perhaps made in response to a letter, an email, or a social media campaign. It's the beginning of potentially something more.
- **In a Relationship:** Gifts of $1,000 or more. This category may include annual donations or monthly giving of $100 or more. Donors at this level believe in your mission and are interested in contributing to your cause on a monthly or annual basis.
- **Part of the Family:** Gifts of $10,000 or more. At this level, the donations are more significant, like larger year-end gifts or matching gifts. Donors at this level feel like they're part of your ministry family. They have a strong connection with you and others involved in your ministry.
- **Long-term Commitment:** Gifts of $100,000 or more. Donors considering this level of contribution are usually looking at significant projects that will have a lasting impact. In my experience, these donors, often with more disposable income, tend to prefer making substantial one-time gifts over monthly contributions. It's important to note that high-dollar donors are more inclined to make outright purchases on your behalf, like a

vehicle or a property, rather than monthly financial contributions.

- **Special Occasions:** Gifts of $1 million or more. Such contributions typically arise during capital campaigns or with large one-time projects. To be ready for a substantial gift like this, your ministry must have a sufficiently ambitious vision. It's crucial to plan and prepare so you don't risk undermining the work you've done or the relationship with the donor by accepting a gift you aren't equipped to handle. If your goal is to attract million-dollar contributions, you'll need to cast a vision that matches this scale.

Why Do People Give?

All this talk of giving begs the question: Why do people give? There can be many different reasons, and you might be surprised that some of them aren't always altruistic. Let's look at the psychological reasons behind why people donate. Donors may not even be aware of these reasons, but you should be. It's important to understand them because they can help you be more strategic in your fundraising and give you new ideas. Here are a few reasons why people give:

1. To feel good about themselves
2. To return a favor
3. To get a tax deduction
4. To solve a problem they find personally important
5. To send a message about their beliefs
6. To align themselves with their friends, peers, or community
7. To bring about justice (or vengeance) where loved ones have been hurt

Let's expound on a few of these points. The first reason listed, "to feel good about themselves," may seem a bit surprising, but if you dig a bit deeper, we've all done this to a certain extent in our lives. Giving a present to someone can feel good. It may not be the main reason we give someone something, but that doesn't mean giving doesn't feel good.

Other times, we give in order to return a favor. In his famous book

Influence: The Psychology of Persuasion, Dr. Robert Cialdini writes about what he calls the Principle of Reciprocity. It states that people are obliged to give back to others in the form of a behavior, gift, or service that they have received first. If a friend invites you to their party, there's an obligation for you to invite them to a future party you are hosting. If a colleague does you a favor, then you owe that colleague a favor. And in the context of a social obligation, people are more likely to say yes to those they owe. It's another form of feeling good, or if we're really honest, absolving ourselves of a feeling of obligation and even guilt.

One of the best demonstrations of the Principle of Reciprocity comes from a series of studies conducted in restaurants. In some restaurants, the waiter or waitress may give you a gift with your bill: a liqueur, a fortune cookie, or perhaps a simple mint. Does the giving of a mint have any influence over how much tip you're going to leave them? Most people will say no. But that mint can make a surprising difference. In the study, giving diners a single mint at the end of their meal typically increased tips by around 3%. People often return favors, whether they realize it or not.

Regarding tax deductions, this goes almost without saying. Individuals and businesses might care about you or your cause, but they also want to lower their tax bill. It's one of the main reasons that year-end giving is so substantial. We'll cover more of this later in chapter 9.

The last few reasons listed above are all similar to each other in some sense. People may care about a certain cause or want to "put their money where their mouth is" regarding their beliefs. In a stronger sense, they may give directly because they see a grave injustice at work or give in a sense of vengeance because they or a loved one has experienced loss. We see that with Mothers Against Drunk Driving and other nonprofits born out of personal tragedy.

Sometimes, we give in order to align ourselves with our peers. How many times have you done something due to peer pressure or group dynamics, simply to align yourself with others? These reactions can be subtle, like dropping money into the offering plate at church because everyone else in your row dropped something in.

Rarely will people support solely because of one of the reasons above.

We want you to be aware of how all these factors come into play. We've met too many missionaries who think support has dried up because God was testing them, because supporters were disobeying God's leading, or some other spiritual reason. Sometimes that's true, and sometimes the reasons are really straightforward.

Next, let's go a bit deeper in understanding a potential donor's level of awareness as it leads into your request for support. This will help you get an idea of the content you should create to address each level of awareness in a way that is organized and effective.

A Prospect's Five Levels of Awareness

Marketing and sales professionals know that there are essentially five levels of awareness that a prospect moves through before they come to a decision on whether to buy or not. We can apply these principles to your fundraising efforts, so let's look at an example that will help unpack this.

When Mike and I were in college (we're about the same age), we both heard a lot from our respective college ministries about the missions movement, particularly through discussion of the 10/40 Window. The 10/40 Window encompasses about seventy countries located between 10 degrees and 40 degrees north latitude. The term was coined by Christian missionary strategist Luis Bush in 1990 to help identify the area of the world least reached by the gospel.

Many college ministry sermons in those days were about the 10/40 Window and how missionaries were needed to reach that region of the world. The sermons were full of stories telling us about the conditions in that part of the world: Many of the countries have multiple languages and dialects. Poverty and illiteracy are ways of life for the majority. Predominant religions include Islam, Hinduism, and Buddhism. There's a large nonreligious block, too.

We were both unaware that such a region existed, but hearing these stories made us aware of the problem. Awareness of the 10/40 Window was further popularized by books like *Revolution in World Missions* by K. P. Yohannan, founder of Gospel for Asia. We read of key insights as to what was going on in those countries and became aware of the need for evangelists to bring the gospel there. This simple example shows us the natural progression that people go through when learning about something new––and what we have to build intentionally if we want others to connect with our work:

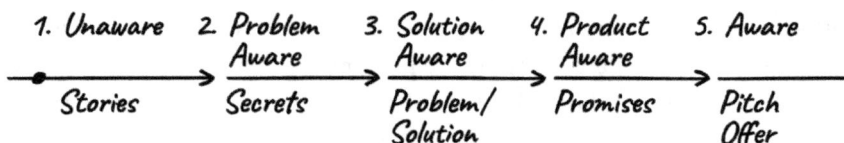

1. Unaware	2. Problem Aware	3. Solution Aware	4. Product Aware	5. Aware
Stories	Secrets	Problem/ Solution	Promises	Pitch Offer

The lowest level of awareness is that a prospect is unaware there is even a problem. To educate the uninitiated, telling stories is often the most important step. This is why we put such a strong emphasis on your stories, covered in chapter 4. Stories ensure you have an opportunity to connect with a prospect no matter what level of awareness they are at. Even the Bible is full of (you guessed it) stories to make people aware of the problem: their need for the gospel.

Once a prospect is problem aware, share insights or "secrets" into what it really takes to create the change needed where you serve. This is exactly what happened through books like *Revolution in World Missions*. Readers learned more about that area of the world and what it would really take to bring the gospel there. They were given special insight into the situation, and this, in turn, made them aware of a solution: an emphasis on world missions and, of course, the gospel.

At this point, the prospect is aware of a solution, and in this case it's simple: the gospel as presented by missionaries sent to the 10/40 Window. At this point, we want to repeatedly emphasize the problem and the solution.

Now, the prospect is product aware (the gospel), and in a sense, the gospel is one big promise: that if you confess your sins and receive Jesus Christ as your Lord and Savior, you'll be granted eternal life. Scripture goes much deeper with the many, many promises God makes to those who receive him, and the offer is, well, to receive Jesus Christ as Lord and Savior. On the fundraising side of things, you'll want to position yourself or your ministry as part of the solution, make promises that the money you raise will go toward accomplishing the vision, and then make your pitch by asking for support. (We'll help you write content for this later in chapter 8, *How to Write a Winning Support Letter.*)

To summarize, when trying to educate college students about the 10/40 Window, pastors and evangelists started by sharing stories. Within just one sermon, it's entirely possible for someone who had never heard of the 10/40 Window to become aware of a problem that they never heard of, learn insights and "secrets" behind fixing that problem, become aware of a solution, and be aware enough to give money or even their life to serve that cause. Keep this in front of you whenever you are writing campaigns:

1. Unaware = Stories
2. Problem Aware = Secrets
3. Solution Aware = Problem / Solution
4. Product Aware = Promises
5. Aware = Pitch (your ask)

Whether written or verbal (we prefer you have both), you should have these five elements of content ready to go: stories, secrets, solutions, promises, and your ask. That way, you'll be ready "in season and out of season" for any interaction. Say you're meeting a potential donor for the first time for coffee. Share a few stories and "secrets" behind what is going on in your field. If you're meeting with a donor who has given to you before, you may just be able to assure them of the progress being made by making promises or even a direct ask. Any good fundraising campaign is going to have all five types of content and repeat them over and over again.

There are plenty of resources online that can help you craft these pieces of content. If you'd like to use the templates and resources we've crafted, consider investing in Fully Funded Academy. Our members have used what they've learned in our training videos and templates to great effect. Visit FullyFundedAcademy.com for more details.

As we close this chapter, here's a little nugget of wisdom: *Show up filled up.* It's a simple saying that packs a lot of punch. Sure, we don't always feel like we're brimming with energy. Lift yourself up in prayer and fill yourself with a sense of purpose. Then walk into that meeting, that conversation, that church, and be a beacon of hope and excitement that draws people in.

Raising support isn't just about what you're doing in the field; it's about the joy and passion you carry into the room or into a conversation.

✦✦✦

Let's get organized! There's a good amount of work to do based on what we've covered in this chapter, but it's so important to do it. You're getting ready to make your ask, so let's get ready.

1. Create and refine your prospect list based on people, churches, or businesses that you know. Jot down those names.
2. At your next team meeting, ask team members for folks they recommend be on your list of prospects.
3. Look through your current donor list and list their giving amount, whether ongoing or one-time. These are folks you already have a closer relationship with. Sort them by their level of commitment and prayerfully consider reaching out to them about increasing their support or giving to a new initiative.
4. Start brainstorming ideas for stories, secrets, solutions, and promises (we'll cover "pitch" later in chapter 8) according to the Five Levels of Awareness we covered. These ideas can serve as a base for future emails, newsletters, and other updates.

To make this easier, download the workbook we've made available for you at FullyFundedAcademy.com. While you're there, consider enrolling in Fully Funded Academy to get even more training, resources, accountability, and coaching so you can get fully funded, faster.

CHAPTER 7

Make Your Difference

Congratulations! If you've made it this far and put some of the concepts we've covered into practice, then you've surely grown in your skills as a fundraiser. We hope and pray that you'll see your hard work pay off and that more money comes in so you can do what you've been called to do.

In my (Mary) early days in fundraising, a mentor told me, "If you want to stay in this industry, you must celebrate the successes." Those words still ring true today. Celebrate the successes, not just for your sake but for your supporters and the people you reach through your ministry.

Sometimes, we're quick to dismiss our victories and move on to the next thing, and we unintentionally overlook those who have helped us get to where we are. Yet one of the most powerful (and repeated) commands we're given in Scripture is to give thanks. Gratitude goes a long way, and in this chapter, we'll cover how to say thank you to those who help you. That way, you'll keep making your difference again and again.

Skipping this step can be a big pitfall. Imagine someone asks you for help and you graciously extend a hand. Afterward, they come right back around to ask for more without thanking you for what you already did. You probably won't feel great, and you'll certainly think twice about helping them again. All too often, this happens in fundraising. Many missionaries come across as transactional simply because they neglect to say thank you. If this goes on too long, they gain the reputation of a "taker," which becomes very difficult to fix.

Learn to Speak Your Supporters' Love Language

When Geno and I got married, we received a copy of Gary Chapman's book, *The 5 Love Languages*. This book was eye-opening, not only in our marriage but also in shaping how I saw my relationships with volunteers and donors. Chapman explains that we each have a "love tank" that must be filled in order to fulfill our desire to be loved. In no particular order, these are the five love languages:

1. Gifts
2. Quality time
3. Words of affirmation
4. Acts of service
5. Physical touch

(You can take Gary's quiz at 5LoveLanguages.com to identify your love language to help you better understand how you give and receive love.) My love language is quality time. Early on in my marriage, I'd often be disappointed when Geno would work in our home office. When he purchased a laptop and started working from the living room, I saw an immediate change in my love tank. It made all the difference to just have him in the same room, which equated to us spending more quality time together. It seems silly, but small gestures like being in the same room together can make a big difference.

Realizing how powerful the love languages are, it became apparent how I could use them to identify the love languages of my volunteers and donors. In most of my fundraising positions, the majority of my time was spent with the volunteer team. These folks were mostly wired for "acts of service," which is why they were volunteering in the first place. I realized that if I expressed my appreciation to them through my own love languages instead of theirs, there would eventually be a disconnect.

To some degree, we all speak each of the five areas, but if you pay a bit of attention, you might be able to pick up cues on the love languages of your volunteers and donors. On the flip side, don't push one particular approach for everyone. If someone says they don't like public recognition, don't force them to get up on stage to receive an award at your next fundraising event. Try your best to recognize your team members in the way that is most appropriate for each person. Or, just incorporate all five love languages into your "thank you plan" and thank them often.

Let's look at a few practical ways you can apply the five love languages to say thank you to your team and donors. Just a note: We included some of the traditional ways larger nonprofits do this. They may not directly translate to your situation, but we're going to list them anyway. We want you to have a broader overview of how these organizations steward relationships well in hopes that it will stir up new ideas for you.

Gifts

- One of your favorite books or journals
- A gift card they can use at their favorite online store
- Digital download of an ebook or audiobook
- A meaningful souvenir from where you serve
- Tickets to a concert
- An award certificate or trophy
- Items with your logo prominently displayed (T-shirts, jackets, mugs, pens, notebooks, journals, motivational books, etc.)
- Flowers
- Special occasion gifts (holidays, birthdays, anniversaries, babies, etc.)
- Personalized content like a photo book (digital or physical) that showcases the work being done, signed by your staff or the people you serve

Quality Time

- One-on-one meetings
- Committee meetings
- Lunch or group gatherings
- Being attentive during each conversation (no distractions or multi-tasking)
- A shared workspace in your office so you have more time together
- Online coffee chats on topics related to your mission work, offering donors the opportunity to learn more and engage directly with you and other team members

Words of Affirmation

- Confirmation that you need them and appreciate their involvement
- Verbal thank you
- Reassurance they are doing a great job
- Phone calls, texts, and social media messages that compliment them for the work they're doing
- Showing you value their opinion by verbally sharing their contributions publicly with others
- Personalized video messages that use video to convey heartfelt thanks, sharing how their contributions have made a difference
- Written or recorded stories showcasing the impact of their support on the community or individuals you serve
- With permission, highlight their contributions on your social media or in your newsletters, making sure to express your genuine appreciation for their support

Acts of Service

- Offer the chance to contribute their skills, whether it's helping with your website, providing online training, or assisting in planning

- Share specific prayer requests related to your mission work, allowing them to serve through prayer
- Offer to help with their volunteer area to ensure they are successful
- Order or purchase materials they have recommended
- Share updates when they cannot attend a group gathering or meeting, and share minutes of the meeting so they don't miss out on important information
- Ensure their area is seen as important and integral to the success of your ministry
- Go out of your way to help during a personal time of need
- Send a gift certificate to a spa day or massage session (service-oriented people tend to shy away from doing nice things for themselves)

Physical Touch

- Handshakes
- High fives or fist bumps
- Hugs
- Patting on the shoulder or back

The News Reporter Strategy

Ask any couple what one of their biggest struggles is and you'll often hear "communication." None of us would ever think a couple who only talks to each other every six months or when one person needs something is a healthy relationship. Any healthy relationship requires communication. Obviously, you're not married to your donors, but you need a consistent communication plan if you're going to continue staying on the field. Whether it's a text, email, phone call, or a quick meetup, simply reaching out can make a big difference.

It's easy to overthink this, but if you remind yourself that your supporters are people first, it can make a big difference. If you're struggling to get started, pretend you're drafting an email with the subject line, "How your dollars are making a difference." It can be a good prompt to get your ideas flowing. If you'd rather record a video with your phone, that could be even easier. "Hey, I'm walking through the hallway of the church that you helped to build! I've only got a few moments, but I want to thank you because you really are making a difference." Or, you could share one real big takeaway from a recent Bible study in the church and then say thanks. It can be that simple.

Don't overlook the reality that most of your supporters may never visit the actual physical location where you serve, so if you simply record a video or write an email from that area, it can go a long way in making them feel like they are there with you. There's a reason why TV reporters still physically go to the scene of the news and broadcast their report from that location. It creates a sense of connection, and the same goes for your supporters. Not everybody is going to be able to join you on-site, but those little messages help supporters feel like they're in it with you because they are!

Because you're heads down in your work day after day, it's easy to think that there isn't really anything special about what you do or where you are. You'll be surprised to realize that there are many things you'd think no one would care about that can make for some wonderful moments for your donors.

Your 7-Step Thank You Plan

Creating a donor stewardship or "thank you" plan ensures that donors don't slip through the cracks. In China, there's a cultural custom of thanking seven times, and this is a good general rule of thumb to follow. Below, you'll find a few ideas on how to do this. Customize these to best connect with your donor and utilize their love language, if possible.

- **Thank You #1:** If a financial gift is made online, an automated email should go out to your donor to confirm their donation and thank them for their gift. If a check was mailed in, a quick phone call within three days from a member of your team should go out to notify them that their check was received, especially if this was a large gift. You don't want your donor to wonder if their donation ever got to your ministry. This eases their mind and shows them that you are organized and value their gift.

- **Thank You #2.** Immediately after receiving a donor's gift, send a brief handwritten thank-you card, preferably from the volunteer or staff member who has the best relationship with that donor. *This is a must.* Sit down and take a few minutes to put into words what their donation has allowed your organization to do. All donations, no matter the size, should receive an immediate thank you. Depending on your relationship with the donor, the medium of that communication may differ.

This goes back to knowing your donor. If you commonly communicate by email, social media, or text, continue to use that medium to immediately respond with excitement and enthusiasm of their support, *but follow it up with a written thank you.* Depending on the level of support, it may be appropriate to consider sending a small commemorative gift as well.

One time, an individual responded to a donation I made by sending me a message saying he was literally doing the happy dance in his living room. That made me so happy! That simple comment made an immediate impression on me as a donor. He expressed excitement and enthusiasm, and I knew I wasn't just another donor. My donation mattered. Don't underestimate the value of sharing that excitement with your donor.

- **Thank You #3:** A phone call or personal letter from the top leader of your ministry within thirty days of receiving the donation. This personal call or letter shows that all levels of your ministry care. It tells your donors they have access to your leadership, and they matter not only to you but to your entire leadership team as well. I encourage you to establish a minimum gift amount here (i.e., $500,

$1,000, $5,000, $10,000) that warrants a call or letter from this individual to ensure they are not overwhelmed with phone calls. In a church, this may be the lead pastor. In a missionary family, this may be the husband or wife who is the primary lead in executing the mission.

- **Thank You #4:** A letter from your advisory group volunteer leader (from chapter 3). Once again, acknowledgement from your leadership shows you are organized and you care at all levels of your ministry.

- **Thank You #5:** A brief thank-you card or letter from your lead volunteer. If this was an event, this thank you may go out from the event chairman, a sub-committee chairman, or a volunteer who oversaw a specific area of the event. A thank you from a non-paid volunteer or an individual you serve will go a long way with your donors.

- **Thank You #6:** Recognize your donors in your newsletters. You may have a monthly, quarterly, bi-annual, or annual newsletter that goes out to all your donors and prospective donors. This is a great way to thank your donors with name recognition or highlight their support in a brief article. Note: if an individual wants to remain anonymous, you can recognize them using the name "Anonymous."

- **Thank You #7:** Recognizing your donor at an upcoming fundraising event is a great way to acknowledge their contribution, even if they aren't there. Donor events come in all shapes and sizes, and we'll go deeper into this in chapter 10. Once again, know your audience. This may be hosted in a home, on-site at a facility they funded, in your office building, a banquet hall, a sponsor's business, etc. It may be a kickoff to the next fiscal year or be hosted in conjunction with a big announcement or a grand total of your most recent fundraising event.

I encourage you to customize the plan for each relationship. With the addition of social media, you should know how to best connect so they know they matter to you and your organization. Remember, they have a choice to give or not to give to your cause. Don't give them any reason not to give.

How Much Should You Share?

When it comes to stewardship and transparency with your donors, there's often a fine line to walk. You might find yourself wondering just how much detail to share about the financial side of things. From my experience, both as a donor and in guiding others in fundraising, the key is to focus on the impact rather than the minutiae of personal finances.

When I contribute to a cause or individual, my primary concern is ensuring my donation is making a difference. If I designate my gift toward a specific project, what I'm really looking for is the outcome of that project. It's about seeing the change my contribution is helping to bring about rather than the specifics of how every dollar is spent on daily living expenses.

Of course, there might be donors who are curious about the nitty-gritty of where their money goes, including personal expenses. However, it's important to remember that donations are meant to support the mission, not to cover personal bills. Share with your supporters the information you're comfortable with, always with an eye toward how it serves the mission they're supporting.

Ultimately, your relationship with your donors is built on trust and shared goals. They're investing in your mission, not in paying your mortgage or car payments. Keeping the focus on the mission and its outcomes reassures your donors that their contributions are indeed making a difference.

Go Change the World

As you continue on your fundraising journey, remember that you play a crucial role in shaping our world! Despite what people think, donations and volunteerism are on the rise, highlighting our innate desire to help others. It's your responsibility as a ministry leader to ensure that your donors see the impact of their contributions clearly.

We hope the steps we've covered over the last several chapters have given you the confidence and direction to raise every dollar needed to say these words: "I'm fully funded!"

We believe in your work to transform lives and encourage you to persevere through the challenges. The world is counting on you and your ministry to make a difference.

Reflect on your vision from chapter 1 and stay focused. While you may not solve all the world's problems, you have a calling to make things better in your area of focus. Celebrate your successes, both big and small, and remember to be grateful for all you have achieved and will achieve.

We've now covered each of the seven steps in our Fully Funded Framework, and we hope you'll come back to them again and again to grow your donor base and raise more support. The last few chapters of this book will serve as practical guides and deeper dives into some of the more important initiatives that undergird your fundraising efforts, including writing a winning support letter, planning your year-end giving campaign, and hosting a fundraising event.

∗∗∗

This chapter has been all about celebrating the wins and saying thank you to your team and supporters. Take these action steps so you can make sure you have a plan to make your difference again and again.

1. Consider taking the 5 Love Languages quiz so you know what your own natural tendencies are and can identify them in others. Visit 5LoveLanguages.com.
2. Use the list of examples we gave you to jumpstart some ideas on how you can say thanks to your team members and current supporters.
3. Create your first "news reporter" piece of content and write or record a special thank you to at least one donor.
4. Work through the 7-Step Thank You Plan and set up reminders to implement it on every new donation that comes in from this point forward.
5. Find a fun way to celebrate your progress so far! No matter where you are in your journey, you have taken significant steps to raising money in a more effective way. Go, you!

Download the workbook we've made available for you at FullyFundedAcademy.com. While you're there, consider enrolling in Fully Funded Academy to get even more training, resources, accountability, and coaching so you can get fully funded, faster.

CHAPTER 8

How to Write a Winning Support Letter

A well-crafted support letter is a vital part of your fundraising strategy. In many instances, it will be one, if not the only, piece of content your potential supporters will truly pay attention to.

There are clear parallels between marketing sales letters and support letters, and I (Mike) want you to understand the principles so you can improve your overall communication. Like the age-old adage says, "Give a man a fish and you feed him for a day. Teach a man to fish and you feed him for a lifetime." In my own way, I want to teach you to fish.

In the marketing world, copywriting is the act of writing text for the purpose of advertising or other forms of marketing. The goal of copywriting is to persuade people to take a specific action. Good copywriting combines the art of storytelling, psychology, and strategic language to create messages that resonate with the target audience. Copywriters write a wide range of content:

- Sales letters
- Emails
- Websites

- Scripts for TV, radio, and online platforms
- Product descriptions and packaging
- Social media posts
- Blog articles with a promotional angle
- Brochures and flyers

One of the big struggles missionaries face in raising funds is the sheer amount of writing involved. While I listed a bunch of things related to marketing above, they aren't that different from the things you've probably found yourself writing. You are already a copywriter!

The Four Non-negotiable Elements of an Effective Support Letter

Copywriting is a skill, which means it can be learned. From this point forward, make sure to weave these four elements into every support letter you write. You do not need to write these sequentially in your letter, but for the sake of diving deeper, I'll cover these concepts in this order:

1. Promise
2. Picture
3. Proof
4. Unique Selling Proposition ("USP" for short)

First, there's the promise you're making about what you're going to do with the money. You want to reassure your donors that funds will be used with integrity. Donors usually aren't looking for a line-by-line review or a chart of accounts. They simply want to see how their donation is connected to the vision fulfilled.

Next, paint a picture of the bigger vision and mission of your campaign. If you did the exercises in chapter 1, work your responses into your support letter so donors can see the bigger vision. Clarify what you do, why you do it, and the transformation that can take place. If you're stuck, answer these questions:

1. What would you do in the next thirty days if you were fully funded?
2. What would you do in the next sixty days after that?
3. The next ninety days after that?
4. For six months after that?

If you total that amount of time, it turns out to be an entire year. It's so easy to get caught up in the day to day that you lose sight of the bigger picture. Visualize what you would do if you were fully funded and guide your donors toward that vision.

Next, provide proof that others vouch for you and your ministry. One way to think of this is to give your donors "the gift of going second." People rarely want to be the first to give, so it's important to help your donors realize that others have supported you and that you have credibility. Keep the phrase "the gift of going second" in mind; you'll see an example of this in the support letter template later in this chapter.

Finally, there's your "unique selling proposition," or USP for short. In the marketing world, the USP is what makes a product stand out from the rest of the competition. In your situation, the USP is what makes you uniquely positioned to make a difference in your specific area or mission field. You want to do more than just pull the "God card" here and tell everyone that "God told me to go to ____." Clearly show why you are uniquely qualified to do the work you've been called to do.

If you apply these principles, you build a compelling case that supporting you and investing in your ministry is a good stewardship of a donor's money. In doing so, you answer the question your donors are asking: "What's in it for me (the donor)?" Let me explain.

WIIFM: "What's In It For Me?"

Truly effective fundraising requires that you put yourself in your donor's shoes. It's not about you! To remember this, abbreviate "What's In It For Me?" to WIIFM and pretend you run a radio station (the "FM" as in "FM radio" always helps me think of this).

Just like a radio station, your goal is to broadcast a frequency that your donor will keep tuning into and find beneficial. Your letters shouldn't just be another ask; they should feel like a meaningful message that your supporters look forward to receiving. This is about creating a partnership that feels rewarding for everyone involved.

Consider the flip side, which sadly happens much too often. Your donors only hear from you once or twice a year and only when you need money. They get your letter in the mail and think to themselves, "Oh great, another support letter from Bob and Sally, whom I haven't heard from the entire year. I bet all they want is money." The letter gets thrown into the trash, unopened.

What's really going on in the mind of the donor? They know there's nothing in the letter for them. Compound this over a number of years and you can see why so many donors stop supporting. It's a never-ending cycle of "gimme, gimme, gimme."

Over the course of time, you'll likely send support letters to the same folks over and over again. At times, you'll need to address uncomfortable questions, like why a certain initiative didn't succeed or why results might be taking longer than expected. You'll encounter setbacks and challenges that will throw a wrench into even the best-laid plans.

In the copywriting and marketing world, we refer to these as objections. All good marketers address a buyer's objections to making a purchase. Likewise, you'll need to address objections people may have about sending you support. At times, they'll have questions about your ministry. Ignoring those objections creates an "elephant in the room" situation where everyone knows something is up, but no one is willing to address anything. You need to address those elephant in the room questions. For example:

- A wealthy businessman is raising money to pay for his $2,000 mission trip to Mexico. The elephant in the room question: "Why doesn't Mr. Multi-Millionaire just pay for his trip himself?"
- A worship leader is trying to raise money to record her fourth worship album. The elephant in the room question: "Shouldn't she have sold enough copies by now to pay for them herself? Maybe she isn't creating very good music!"

- A missionary is raising money for yet another church plant, his fifth in five years. None of the other churches still exist. What's the elephant in the room objection? "Maybe this guy isn't very good at church planting."

Ask yourself, "What is the biggest objection someone could have to giving to you?" If you're not comfortable being open, then donors won't feel comfortable opening their wallets. The examples earlier were more extreme, so let's look at a few that might be more applicable to your situation. We led our students through these exercises, and the following are a few objections they came up with:

- "We're serving in the United States, and that's not a real mission field."
- "Why don't you just get a real job?"
- "Why don't you work part-time to support yourself, like Paul did tentmaking?"
- "You're raising support so you can live in a prayer ministry and just pray all day? Shouldn't you do something more practical?"
- "The place you're doing ministry is a vacation spot. Why should I support you so you can live on an island?"
- "You're only doing administrative work and no hands-on ministry with people. Shouldn't the organization you work for pay you rather than you raise your own support?"

Obviously, no one said this directly to these missionaries, but I can almost guarantee their supporters have thought it to themselves at some point. It takes courage to think through the objections people may have, but if you do, you'll attain a level of clarity you may not have had before.

It's easy to cloak things in spiritual or vague language. We encourage you not to do that. A common phrase that many use as a crutch is "we are in transition"—that's fine, but if you're always in transition and never building anything, people are going to have real objections.

An Actual Support Letter

Some time ago, a friend named Kent hired me to write a support letter for his church plant. At the time, Kent and his wife, Gina, left a full-time position leading a campus ministry and felt called to plant a church in Boston. One of the big "elephant in the room" issues is that they asked for support to plant the church three years earlier, but it had still not been launched. Now, they were asking for more support. For the campaign to be effective, I felt they needed to address this, especially because they wanted to raise an additional $30,000.

This approach paid off, as they quickly surpassed their fundraising target in a few weeks. Read the letter below in its entirety. For the sake of clarity, I kept their stories and details in there but also put blanks in for your own information. Hundreds of missionaries have used this letter as a template for their own support letters and experienced incredible results. (You have our permission to do so.) Download the workbook we've made available for free at FullyFundedAcademy.com.

***

Dear [NAME],

In over 14 years of ministry, my wife, [SPOUSE's NAME], and I have given our lives to pastor and mentor those whom God has sent us to. For the past 3 years, the Lord planted us in the Boston area, specifically Cambridge. On [LAUNCH DATE]: we are formally launching [MINISTRY NAME]!

What have we been doing for the past 3 years?

The past few years have been vital in assimilating into Cambridge life. Though we held church services and did outreach, [WIFE] and I approached ministry here as missionaries. We focused on building relationships, then adapted our training and past experience to minister in this unique community. We essentially learned a new way of life.

Launching earlier would have been premature. The right team had to be trained, church infrastructure and leadership had to be built, and resources needed to be gathered. Now, after 3 years of diligent training, building, and saving—we are ready!

Welcome home, Cambridge.

Cambridge, Massachusetts, is like no other place on Earth. It's an academic and political hotbed — home to some of the world's top universities, including Harvard University and MIT. To say Cambridge is influential is an understatement. Eight US presidents have graduated from Harvard alone. MIT boasts 81 Nobel laureates! One in three people in Cambridge are from another country.

We are going to launch [MINISTRY NAME] right in the heart of this influential and diverse community.

That's why our team is calling this the "Welcome Home" campaign. We want to bring people home: to Christ, to eternity, and to God's family.

Opposition awaits. We've all heard the Northeast is the "preacher's graveyard." A biblical worldview wars against the intellectual ideologies that are prevalent here. Yet we've determined to make [MINISTRY NAME] home to the people of Cambridge. Our goal is to have 150–180 new people attend our launch. Then, we'll continue with our weekly services in strength.

We are uniquely qualified and called to reach this community.

- We know Cambridge. We've lived here, worked here, and raised our kids here.

- Our past college ministry experience has been vital in helping us understand student life and building relationships with people from diverse backgrounds.

- Our team is talented and diverse and has caught the vision to reach this city.

- I've personally called on top church planters to advise and train us. My mentors have been with us every step of the way.

- We have the support of other local pastors. Our heart is to reach Cambridge . . . together.

Would you give financially to launch [MINISTRY NAME]?

[WIFE NAME] and I have already given to this launch. I have been working a day job to supplement the ministry's income. Balancing time and energy is a sacrifice, but we're completely sold out to this vision.

Would you join us in giving to the launch of [MINISTRY NAME]?

Our goal is to raise $30,000 over the next three months. Our deadline: [DEADLINE DATE].

[page break]

Our Financial Breakdown:

- $8,000—This will help [WIFE NAME] and I devote ourselves to leading [MINISTRY NAME] full-time. We will spearhead the launch, build ministry infrastructure, cultivate relationships with the Cambridge community, and equip leaders until [MINISTRY NAME] is self-sustaining.

- $8,000—Marketing. This includes print materials, direct mailers, a website revamp, and securing bus and subway ad space. Part of the challenge in an urban environment is being seen and heard above the noise. We want to meet students where they're at: online and on the subway.

- $5,000—Outreach. We love serving our Cambridge community, but it costs money. We will engage in 3–4 large-scale community outreach initiatives between now and September to build stronger relationships and gain exposure.

- $5,000—Mobile church equipment. This includes tech gear (microphones, cables, other worship equipment) and service equipment, like seats and tables.

- $4,000—Unforeseen expenses. This will go toward hospitality, unforeseen needs, last-minute expenditures, and discipleship needs after the launch.

Individual one-time donations.

This is an individual breakdown of what we would need to reach our financial goal. Would you take one of these slots?

- 8 people at $1000

- 12 people at $500

- 15 people at $250

- 20 people at $100

If you prefer to give toward specific needs, access our faith list at [YOUR DONATE PAGE].

Your gift will be handled with complete integrity through the 501(c)(3) organization of [MINISTRY NAME] and under the accountability of our external ministry overseers, including Pastor [NAME] from [CHURCH] in [CITY, STATE,] and Pastor [NAME] from [CHURCH] in [CITY, STATE].

In closing . . .

Our goal is not just a one-time event or a blip on the screen. We've diligently prepared our team for the long haul. We're here to make disciples of Christ in Cambridge. [MINISTRY NAME] will be a life-giving, impact church . . . with your help.

Help us launch a life-giving church in the heart of one of the most influential communities in the world. Help us launch [MINISTRY NAME]. Help us bring the people of Cambridge . . . home.

Sincerely,

[YOUR NAME]

[TITLE, MINISTRY]

✱✱✱

Never Waste a Subheading

Let's dive into the nuts and bolts of this letter. The first thing I want to point out is the importance of the subheadings throughout. Most people will not read your letter from start to finish. Rather, they will scan the subheadings first. If a subheading is clear, informative, and compelling, they will skim the other subheadings. If enough of what they skim is interesting, they'll go back and re-read the letter from start to finish.

You need to make your subheadings count. The rule of thumb is that someone should be able to get the gist of your entire message solely by reading the subheadings. If we list all the subheadings in this letter, this is what it reads:

- What have we been doing for the past 3 years?
- Welcome home, Cambridge.
- We are uniquely qualified and called to reach this community.
- Would you give financially to launch [MINISTRY NAME]?
- Our Financial Breakdown:
- Individual one-time donations.
- Help us launch a life-giving church in the heart of one of the most

influential communities in the world. Help us launch [MINISTRY NAME]. Help us bring the people of Cambridge . . . home.

All of these subheadings were written with intention. It allows folks who just want to quickly get the point to acquire the information they need while also allowing those who are more detail-oriented to truly dive into what Kent is doing and why. Once you see these copywriting principles at work, it's hard to "unsee" them. Let's dig a bit deeper.

The letter starts with a strong opening. I specifically mention fourteen years because it builds proof that Kent and Gina aren't just some fly-by-night folks who were going about this endeavor casually. I wanted to establish this upfront because we were going to address what they had been doing the past three years. Then, I was specific with where they felt called to serve and named the city of Cambridge.

Here's a powerful writing tip: Be specific enough to be believable and universal enough to be relevant. When possible, you want to name things like people and places. When possible, give dates and numbers. Specifics make things sound more believable. Compare these two statements: "We are going to reach the world for Christ" versus "We are going to plant a church in the Boston area, specifically Cambridge." The second is clearly better because the specificity creates a sense of purpose and paints a picture of where they'll serve, even if a reader has never been to the Boston area.

The Elephant in the Room: "What have we been doing the past 3 years?"

We address the elephant in the room right off the bat. I chose to do this because Kent told me that most of the people he was reaching out to for support had previously donated in the past. I wanted to show his readers there were clear reasons why the church had not been launched right away (I use the word "premature") and how he spent his time during those few years.

Clearly, Kent and Gina were very active, but oftentimes, donors will look solely at the results rather than the process. It was important to show that he wasn't squandering the money that had been donated and that he was using it to lay the groundwork for the church.

Picture: "Welcome home, Cambridge."

In this section, I was intent on creating an image in the reader's mind of the stakes at hand. If his readers weren't familiar with Cambridge before, they would be now because Harvard and MIT are famous universities. I researched the people who graduated from those schools to show that the church was being planted in a place of influence. I also show what kind of opposition awaits, using language like "the preacher's graveyard" and how the ideologies there "war" with a biblical worldview.

Finally, I close this section with more specifics by sharing the number of people they were hoping to have for their launch. When you set a clear target, people are more likely to help you hit it. All of these writing tactics help raise the stakes.

Make Your First Ask "Before the Fold"

All of this takes place on the first page of the support letter, "before the fold." The concept of "the fold" comes from the traditional newspaper layout, where the most important news is placed on the upper half of the front page, ensuring it's visible when the paper is folded. In a support letter, "the fold" refers to the point at which the letter would be folded, usually meaning the bottom of the first page.

Making your first ask before the fold leverages a crucial window of engagement and respects your reader's time and attention. Obviously, if your letter is sent digitally, it will be hard to get to the ask so quickly before they make the first scroll on their device, which is why the subheadings are so important in keeping your reader's attention.

I share Kent and Gina's unique qualifications for serving in that area and use "the gift of going second" concept by sharing that they themselves have already contributed. There's more specificity by listing the clear dollar amount of $30,000 and the timeframe of three months. All of this is intentional.

The Second Page

It's up to you whether you want to break down giving amounts for your readers or not. In this case, I felt it wise to promise readers that there was a clear plan to make this launch a success. All of the bullet points support this premise. As for individual donations, I broke them down into increments by doing the math to make it easy for individuals to see where they could fit into the overall plan.

The section saying, "Your gift will be handled with complete integrity through the 501(c)(3) organization," is yet another use of the concept of "giving the gift of going second" and proof that there is oversight and accountability. The letter closes with a passionate appeal and one more ask.

Where Are the Pictures?

Many of our Fully Funded Academy members have asked whether they should put pictures in their support letters. There's no hard and fast rule, but we typically advise that it's better to communicate clearly in the letter and attach pictures to the letter elsewhere inside the envelope. Having pictures in the support letter takes up valuable real estate, creates a lot of design headaches that waste your time, and can distract readers from reading the actual letter. If you're sending your letter via email, then you can always attach pictures in the body of your email and encourage donors to read the letter separately.

We've covered many important things in this chapter, from understanding donor psychology, constructing a narrative that resonates, and strategically placing our ask to maximize engagement. Remember that the power of a support letter lies not just in its words but in the authenticity and clarity it conveys about your mission. Each letter is an opportunity to connect deeply with the hearts and minds of those who share your passion and to invite them into the story you are living out every day.

Let your support letters be the bridge that brings your donors closer to the impact they can make alongside you. Write not just for the moment but for the movement you are building, knowing that every word you write carries the potential to bring change to lives.

✳✳✳

The support letter template is available as part of the free workbook, which you can download at FullyFundedAcademy.com. While you're there, consider enrolling in Fully Funded Academy to get even more training, resources, accountability, and coaching so you can get fully funded, faster. Happy writing!

CHAPTER 9

How to Plan Your Year-End Campaign

In 2016, I (Mike) bought my first house, nestled in the small New Jersey town where I went to high school. The house itself was a fresh build, but since the builders were trampling all over the yard during construction, the lawn was just a stretch of bare dirt, both in the front and back. A landscaper explained that to get the lush, green lawn I always dreamed of, I'd need to care for it through the seasons for a full year. That is not what I wanted to hear! Part of me wondered why I couldn't just water the seeds nonstop and have the grass grow full in a week.

Obviously, nature doesn't work that way. You can't just flood grass seeds with water and expect a great lawn overnight. Doing so would actually kill it. Growing a healthy lawn isn't something you can rush. Patience, time, and the right actions at the right moments are key. The same goes for your fundraising campaigns.

There Is a Season for Everything, Including Marketing

Ecclesiastes 3:1 says, "To everything there is a season, and a time to every purpose under the heavens" and it seems that even marketers have taken this to heart. Seasonal marketing is a strategic approach that aligns campaigns with the natural ebb and flow of seasons, holidays, and significant events throughout the year. For example, we're all aware that it's likely we'll see a ton of ads for Valentine's Day in February, Mother's Day in May, "back-to-school" promotions in August and September, and, of course, the holiday season between Thanksgiving and Christmas. The good news for you is that a seasonal marketing approach can take a huge weight off your shoulders and make it easy to create content to communicate with your donors.

By aligning your campaigns with moments already marked as special in your audience's lives, you tap into their heightened sense of community, generosity, and openness to engagement. This not only makes your message more relevant but also feels less intrusive because it aligns with the rhythm of your donors' daily lives.

More specifically, year-end fundraising stands out as a pivotal opportunity for several reasons. The closing months of the year, especially from November through December, are traditionally times of reflection, gratitude, and giving back. There's a huge collective push toward generosity, making people more receptive to appeals for support. People love giving gifts at this time of year. The numbers vary from year to year, but we've seen statistics that report as high as 32 percent of all donations are given during this season, adding up to about $1.23 billion!

The most recent numbers show that folks aged forty to sixty-four are the ones opening their wallets the most, donating around $2,500 a year to causes they care about. This age group usually has a bit more in the bank. They're in their peak earning years, and some have retirement on the horizon, making them think more about where their money can do some good. These numbers may change depending on when you read this, but not even the COVID pandemic in 2020 drove these numbers down. Moreover, the end of the tax year adds a practical incentive for individuals and businesses to make donations. This is all great news for you!

To run a successful year-end campaign, you need two key elements: knowing *what* to say and knowing *when* to say it. In essence, you need a solid content plan that outlines your message and a calendar that schedules the timing for each communication. Let's work backward and start with the calendar first. When we start with the end in mind, we can follow one course until success (FOCUS).

Your Year-End Fundraising Calendar

It's easy to assume that a year-end campaign should start at year's end, but if you want to have a successful campaign, you need to start watering the lawn much earlier. We recommend starting in August and ending with the final week of December. Here's a quick and easy content plan:

- **August:** content email every two weeks
- **September:** content email every two weeks
- **October:** content email every two weeks
- **November:** one content email and a financial recap letter
- **December:** one content email, your support letter, and one follow-up email

Let's go month by month, then I'll provide a few specific topics you can potentially write about. August is a great time to wrap up the summer, touching base with supporters to share what's been happening. Think of this as catching up with friends. One email should recap some of the things you did over the summer regarding the ministry. Another email could be about something you or your family did during the summer.

September has strong associations with new beginnings. Students typically go back to school, and those in the workforce trade in the summer travel mindset to get to work. Even new sports seasons like football start at this time of the year. Since people are already thinking about fresh starts, use these themes to connect with your audience.

October typically reminds most people of autumn. Focus on content that adds value to your supporters, even if it's not tied directly to your ministry. Think of these emails as a way to keep the conversation going, offering something worthwhile in each message as you build momentum toward the end of the year.

If your donors live in the United States, November is all about Thanksgiving. We recommend sending your correspondence the first and third week of the month so you can work around the Thanksgiving holiday. The first one could be a simple email about the power of gratitude and how you practice it. During the third week, right before Thanksgiving, send out a financial recap letter. We'll cover the nuts and bolts of this letter at the end of this chapter.

In December, we recommend sending three pieces of content. Your first should be an email about Christmas. Your second piece should be your support letter (which we covered in the last chapter), sent out the week before or week of Christmas. The final piece should be a follow-up ask for support, sent right after Christmas so it reaches supporters during that important window between December 26 and December 31. During this time, many are reflecting on the past year and planning their final contributions. It's your opportunity to make one more ask, with the hope and goodwill of the season on your side.

Exactly What to Say (Sort Of)

Let's look at a few sample topics you could write to your list about based on the calendar above. Before you dive in, it's important to note that not every piece of correspondence should be about you or the ministry.

Remember the "WIIFM" concept we covered in the last chapter. To build a good relationship with donors, it's important for you to add value to them and not make every correspondence just about your work or the money you need. You know more helpful things than you may think!

Imagine you're sending out an email with "Five Things Your Spouse Needs to Hear You Say" as the subject line. The content could include some lessons you've learned about communication, empathy, and resolving conflict. If you're not married, no sweat! Change the subject to "Five Things Your Friends Need to Hear You Say" and share the same lessons.

Every single donor you know has friends, colleagues, or family in their lives. You're a missionary; you probably talk to more strangers in a year than your donors will in a lifetime! You know things, friend. Share your insights and add value to your donors. This content might not directly relate to your mission work, but at the end of the email you can include a simple "P.S. Thank you for your support this year." The goal is to show your supporters that emails from you aren't just requests for money or ministry updates. You're nurturing a deeper, longer-lasting connection with them.

August:

1. Summer Recap: 3 Amazing Things You Helped Us Accomplish
2. Behind the Scenes: A Few Personal Updates

September:

1. My Personal Recs: Helpful Resources about Starting New Seasons
2. How to Blend Your Spiritual and Work Life (Without Being Preachy)

October:

1. 5 Things Your Spouse Needs to Hear You Say
2. How I Pack for Any Trip (In Less than Ten Minutes!)

November:

1. This Gratitude Practice Changed My Life
2. [YEAR] Financial Recap—THANK YOU!

December:

1. Personal Touches to Make Your Christmas Extra Special
2. Our Vision for the Year 20xx (please read!)
3. Can you help?

While this content plan provides a structured approach to your year-end fundraising campaign, it's not written in stone. Remember, the key is to add value and stay in touch. Just seeing subject lines like this can get your creative juices flowing, and you can still weave in your own personal stories or references to your ministry.

For instance, a headline about packing can transition into a reflection on your life as a missionary, sharing practical tips from your experiences of being constantly on the move. Similarly, a message about making Christmas special could include insights into how the holiday season is celebrated in the country where you serve compared to the country where your donor base is located. This blend of planning and personal storytelling makes your communication meaningful and relatable while still giving readers a glimpse into your world.

Here are a few other topics you might write about (these are among the most popular that our students in Fully Funded Academy have used):

- 12 Relational Mistakes You Don't Know You're Making
- Three Laws in [city or country you serve] You Didn't Know About
- How to Confront Someone without Being a Jerk
- Seven of My Favorite Resources for Bible Study
- How to Pack in Five Minutes
- 10 Evangelism Hacks: A Cheat Sheet to Bringing up Christ in a Conversation
- 12 Things Your Kids Won't Tell You (But Might Want To)
- My Review of [name a book, app, or resource]
- Why I Am No Longer _ _ _ _ (this is to explain a decision you've made)

Those who have invested the time to create content like this have reported incredible results, not just financially but because of the shift in mindset they've made. They've made the transition from someone in need to someone who operates from a place of abundance and adding value. One of the most helpful things a missionary told me in my youth was, "Don't just live for God, live from God. Realize that He is your Father and you have access to all the resources He does." It changed the way I looked at the world, and especially money.

Friend, you have value to add, not just to the people you serve but to the donors who are supporting your work. Don't forget about them! If you take the time to add value, you will experience incredible things.

The Financial Recap Letter

One of the pieces of content we recommend having ready is a Financial Recap Letter. This allows you to shift the communication to finances during your campaign. Feel free to use this at a different time during the year if it aligns with other campaigns.

Being transparent about your finances, whether you're celebrating successes or acknowledging challenges, speaks volumes. It shows you're stewarding their support wisely and invites them to be part of your ongoing journey.

Does this mean diving into specifics like salaries and expenses? Sure, if you're comfortable. But the key is to share progress and vision. This is more about helping your donors see that they're backing a cause that's making a real impact and that you are stewarding your resources well. Typically, we advise that this is a two-page letter. If you have a website, you can put the entire letter on one web page.

***

Page One:

[month], 20XX

Dear Friend,

As we wind down another year, I'm more convinced than ever that God is at work through the initiatives here in [your location] and that [your ministry], together with you, is answering this call.

One of the central themes of Scripture is to "go and make disciples of all nations." This call is manifested in so many ways. Some serve in local churches, others fight poverty, alleviate hunger, or provide for felt needs. Still others do the more unconventional, such as translating Scripture for remote people groups.

For us, we obey the call by [state what you do]. As we work to respond to these needs, we rely on God's provision and your generosity. We are grateful for yet another year in which we have been able to do so much on behalf of the people whom we serve.

This past year, our overall support grew by [how much] percent. We are grateful for you and our other partners—individuals, churches, and other donors—who equip us to provide a full range of services to help transform lives in [your location].

This past year [share an interesting stat like "we installed 47 clean water pumps in coastal villages"].

- [share an interesting stat like "we distributed 325 winter coats and 900 lbs of rice"].

- [share an interesting stat like "we've seen 29 people come to Christ this past year"].

Jesus often ministered in places where others were reluctant to go, serving and ministering often to the rejected and overlooked.

We still feel the call to serve here in [your location], and we're excited about the initiatives we have planned for the coming year, which you can get a glimpse of on the second page of this letter.

Thank you for partnering with us. We are so grateful for your partnership in expression of the Great Commission!

Blessings,

[Your Name]
[Your Title, organization]

Page Two:

Financial Highlights for 20XX

We strive to be financially accountable to our donors and the communities we serve. All of our finances are handled with complete integrity through the 501(c)(3) organization [your agency or sending church]. Any further inquiries can be sent to [your email address or contact person's email address].

Revenue Sources

Individual Donations	$xxxx.xx
Church Monthly Support	$xxxx.xx
Gifts-In-Kind*	$xxxx.xx
Other Income	$xxxx.xx
Total:	$xxxx.xx

*The "Gifts-In-Kind" category denotes gifts donated in lieu of cash and is calculated to estimate cash value. In 20XX, these gifts included a new laptop computer, a donated pick-up truck, plane tickets to travel home for furlough, and the like.

Operating Expenses

Cost-of-Living	$xxxx.xx
Ministry Expenses	$xxxx.xx
Fundraising	$xxxx.xx
Total:	$xxxx.xx

Our Goals for Next Year In 20XX, our goal is to continue bringing aid [or whatever it is your ministry does] to the people of [location]. While we understand that "neither the one who plants nor the one who waters is anything, but only God, who makes things grow" (1 Corinthians 3:7), our aim is to keep overhead low and be good stewards of the seed we have. We endeavor to[something on your heart to do (i.e., plant one more church along the coast)].

- [increase the number of coats we donate by 20 percent].

- [train X number of local leaders to carry on the work].

We are always trying to be faithful stewards of the work God has given to us and the financial support and resources you have entrusted to us.

In a few short weeks, we will send you our final support letter for the calendar year. Our hope is that you will partner with us in this next season to further the work here in [location].

You **are** making a difference—and we thank you!

In Christ,

Your Name

✱✱✱

Remember, openness fosters trust. This letter is all about striking a balance that builds confidence among your supporters. By proactively sharing your financial journey, you're not just keeping your donors informed—you're inviting them into a deeper level of engagement with your mission. You never know what positive outcomes might unfold from this! It could be the catalyst for someone with substantial skills to offer their expertise to help refine your strategies or to give a larger year-end gift.

***

The Financial Recap Letter template is available as part of the free workbook, which you can download at FullyFundedAcademy.com. While you're there, consider enrolling in Fully Funded Academy to get even more training, resources, accountability, and coaching so you can get fully funded, faster.

CHAPTER 10

How to Host a Group Fundraising Event

When it comes to actual face-to-face fundraising, three approaches come to mind. You're familiar with all three because they mirror how ministry often happens:

1. One-on-one meeting
2. Small group gathering
3. Large event

The first is similar to one-on-one discipleship, the second is like a small group or Bible study, and the third is like a church service. All three are important, but we've found that most missionaries often overlook the second option.

While one-on-one meetings are powerful and effective, they don't always happen. Both you and your donors are strapped for time, and if you're home on furlough and trying to raise funds, running around to a bunch of one-on-one meetings can be difficult to coordinate. When it comes to large events, most missionaries think of this as sharing about their ministry during a Sunday service at a church or preaching at their home church. If you're like any of the missionaries we've coached, you've likely found it difficult to secure those kinds of opportunities on an ongoing basis, if at all.

You've got a lot of money to raise, and relying just on face-to-face meetings or hoping for a rare opportunity to speak at church isn't always going to be enough. Sure, there's something special about one-on-one interactions, but when it comes to reaching out to people who might not know you very well, a one-on-one coffee meet-up might come off as a bit daunting. They might hesitate, wondering why they should spend time with someone they're not too familiar with.

Instead, invite them to a gathering where they'll be among others and share in a collective experience. Suddenly, the idea doesn't seem so formal or pressure-filled. It's simply an invitation to learn about the work you're passionate about in a relaxed, welcoming environment. That's why we're such big fans of leveraging small group gatherings and hosting a fundraising event.

This Is Just Like Every Holiday Party or Weekend BBQ You've Attended

Imagine gathering your family and friends for a warm Thanksgiving meal, a cozy Christmas dinner, or even a fun-filled summer barbecue. That's exactly the spirit we're aiming to capture with your fundraising event. There's no need to overcomplicate things or get too caught up in the planning.

We recommend aiming for ten to thirty attendees with the intent to bring people together, allowing them to connect, and then sharing the journey of your ministry. To that end, simply think of these before planning an event:

- Who
- What
- Where
- When
- Why

Let's start with "who" because this approach allows you to host different groups of people.

As the old saying goes, "Birds of a feather flock together." You could host one event with folks from your home church, another with friends you want to catch up with, and still another with a corporate leader or business owner who can bring their own friends or connections to meet you. If you feel like mixing your social circles could be awkward, this is the perfect remedy!

Holding this event isn't about casting a wide net and inviting anyone who will come. It's about carefully choosing a select group of people to join you. Think about how it feels to receive an invitation to a party or a wedding. It's special, right? You know the host has a limited number of spots, and they picked you to fill one of them. That feeling of being personally chosen is exactly the vibe we're aiming for with this gathering. It's not just any event; it's an intimate, invitation-only thing.

The second step is to think through *what* kind of event you'd like to host. If it's with church folks, a simple backyard BBQ on a Sunday afternoon after church might work great. With your friends, a dinner hosted at a friend's house would be a good option. With businesspeople, your best bet might be to reserve a back room for dinner at a restaurant where things can be more formal and private. Be thoughtful about what would make your attendees comfortable.

Where you host the event will be tied closely to the "who" and the "what" because people who are closer to you already might prefer meeting in a home, whereas businesspeople and their colleagues might be turned off by that idea. Some of our members in Fully Funded Academy have told us they were able to meet in meeting rooms in their workplace (with permission, of course) during a lunch break.

Others we've worked with have less of a direct ministry focus and more of a cause-based focus (think of our friend James Harrington, who runs the Ugandan Water Project, or Rob Morris with Love146) that allows them to secure meeting spaces in their town for free and invite business owners and other pillars in the community. In James's case, it might be a bad idea to host the event at a church since attendees may go to different churches or not at all. Each situation is different, but what is common is that there is forethought, intention, and action taken in order to make this happen.

As for when you host the event, a big part of this will depend on the previous factors. If it's church people, a Sunday evening or a weeknight might work well, but consider avoiding Monday night (people are typically frazzled by the start of the work week) or a Friday or Saturday night, as they or their families may have plans. If you're inviting couples who have kids, consider whether they'll need to get babysitting or not.

If you're gathering different groups, you might simply ask one or two on your guest list what works best for them. Some of our members have been surprised by the responses and ended up doing brunch on a Saturday, which they found people could attend because attendees were able to come by after dropping their kids off at tutoring, sports, or music lessons at the start of the day.

You don't always have to base your event around a particular meal either. Several have reported that a 7:00 p.m. or 7:30 p.m. time can also work great because it gives them enough time to get home from work, have dinner, put their kids down, and hop over for dessert and tea. People you know from church may well be accustomed to this time since Bible study groups or mid-week services often start around that time.

If you enlist a team like we talked about in chapter 3, some of your team members may be willing to host this event for you or help with the costs or preparation of food. The possibilities really are endless. It's a great way for your team to feel invested in your work and step out to help you.

How to Invite People to Your Event

When inviting people to your event, remember that you want to make it feel special. This isn't an "open to anyone and everyone" gathering, but that doesn't mean you can't take a simple approach to it.

If you're inviting friends and family, inviting people to your event can be super straightforward. It might be a quick Facebook message, a text, or even just a call to let them know you'd love their company. Think about how you invite family over for Thanksgiving. In both of our families, we have a group chat that we use for everything. Naturally, that's what we'd use to send out the invite. It's all about finding the best way to reach your crowd. If you usually text each other, then a text invite is perfect. But if the occasion calls for something a bit more formal, don't hesitate to send out a proper invitation.

Let's look at a few examples from real-life invitations our members have sent out. This first one is from a young man hosting a fundraising event where he gathered friends, family, and a few special individuals. In this case, it was one of his high school teachers whom he contacted through Facebook Messenger. (Before you read it, we should mention that "Boston butt" is a kind of slow-smoked pulled pork. It's funny to read, but that was this particular guy's kind of humor and why he said it that way!)

> *Hey, Mrs. Lamb, I'm getting together with some friends on Thursday, March 8, in Camilla to share some exciting updates about our ministry work. We'll be having some really good Boston butt, sides, and dessert. I'd love for you and Mr. Joe to be there. We'll start at 6:30 and be done by 8:00 p.m.*

He used very formal language ("Mrs. Lamb") because she's a teacher. This was perfect for his scenario and the type of gathering he was hosting.

A Simple Text Invitation

When sending an invitation to closer friends and in a less formal manner, this was used:

> *Hey, I'm getting some friends together Thursday evening in Camilla to catch up. I'll also share a bit about what we're doing with our ministry.*

> *I know your schedule is pretty busy, but would you happen to be in town this Thursday?*

A Standard Invitation

An invitation sent through email or private message through social media could read like this:

(Ministry Logo)

March 8, 20XX
6:30 p.m.
Camilla Hall

Join us for an evening of fellowship, coffee, desserts, and ministry updates.

Please RSVP to (XXX) XXX-XXXX.

How to Use Your Event to Reconnect with Those Who Can't Attend

This next example shows how you can use an event to connect with people locally and also how you can use the momentum and energy around it to reconnect with folks who are out of town or no longer in the area. This is a perfect way to reach out to show people you're thinking of them, even if you know they can't attend.

> Hey, Pastor Gary, I was thinking about you and your family and wanted to share with you the exciting news that I'm now working with (Name of Ministry).
>
> I'm hosting a meetup here locally to share more, but I see you guys moved to Texas. That's exciting. I hope the church is doing well and that you're enjoying a fruitful ministry. Since you're not here locally, meeting for dinner wouldn't be very feasible, but I'd love to give you guys a call and catch up.
>
> Would next Tuesday or Thursday at 2 p.m. or 3 p.m. Central work for you? Hope to talk to you soon.

A More Formal Invitation

For a more formal gathering, let's look at an event I hosted in St. Louis for Inner City Ministries.

- **Who:** Other pastors in the city
- **What:** Breakfast
- **Where:** Our facility in the city
- **When:** Tuesday, March 1 at 7:30 a.m.
- **Why:** To raise awareness and funds for a church planting project in the inner city

The strategy was simple: Call first, then send the formal invite. We had four total people on the team: Pastor Brian, two other influential pastors in the city, Jared and Jerry, and myself. Since we were inviting pastors to this breakfast, we wanted to make the invitations personal. Pastors are quite busy and can be hard to get a hold of. The personal touch would ensure the invitation wasn't coming out of the blue. If the lead pastor couldn't make it, we'd ask for the assistant pastor. The goal was to ensure each church from the area was represented.

We requested an RSVP by February 26 to keep tabs on the breakfast headcount. We made it hassle-free to respond and invited them to text, call, or email at their convenience.

We drew up our guest list, and the first outreach was to make phone calls to each person on our list. Since I was coordinating the campaign, I first sent an email to our other team members, pastors Jared and Jerry, to make things easier for them when reaching out.

> *Good morning, Jared and Jerry!*
>
> *Thanks again for all your help to ensure we have a great turnout at the ICM launch on March 1. We're good to host the launch breakfast at the Inner City Ministries building on March 1 at 7:30 a.m. Below are some notes for your calls this week.*
>
> *I've also included the proof of the invitation. Please take a minute to look it over and let me know if you have any edits before we go to print today. Jared, I'll send you a separate email with your call list with the addresses and phone numbers.*

If they give you a different address, just jot it down and send it my way. Let me know if you have any questions or thoughts on the invitation. We're looking forward to a great event on March 1 and appreciate you guys so much. Have a great day.

Warmly,

Mary

Here is the call script I sent to them:

Hi, may I speak with Pastor (name)?

(If he/she is NOT available, ask for the pastor's assistant and share the information below with him/her.)

(If he/she is available) Hi Pastor (name),

So great to connect with you. I wanted to be sure to give you a heads-up that I mailed you an invitation for breakfast on March 1 to hear more about Inner City Ministries of St. Louis.

We'll be meeting up at the Inner City Ministries building at 7:30 a.m. We are working on getting a headcount and wanted to see if you'll be able to join us.

(If yes) Great! We look forward to seeing you there. You can go ahead and park on the side of the building, and we'll be in the main building.

(If no) We completely understand. Is there another time we could schedule to get together for coffee or at your office?

(If yes, schedule the appointment.)

(If no, ask if you can follow up to share how the event went and you can find a time to meet then.)

For invitations, we took advantage of the services at Vistaprint.com. The process was simple: choose a design, pop in a logo, and fill in the details. For just about $20, we had over a hundred classy invitations in our hands in no time.

The cherry on top was featuring the names of all three pastors, Brian, Jerry, and Jared, right on the invitation. This gave the event an incredible boost of credibility.

Imagine this: You're a lead pastor in the city. The message is that Reverends Jared, Jerry, and Brian warmly invite you to the launch of Inner City Ministries. The date is set for Tuesday, March 1—a breakfast meeting to chat about the biggest church planting project the city has ever seen. Sounds like an event you wouldn't want to miss, especially knowing it will be a gathering of peers and friends, right?

If we didn't get an RSVP by the deadline, I'd follow up with a gentle reminder call. This is just a friendly nudge, saying, "Hey, it's Mary, calling on behalf of Reverend Jared. Just checking in to see if you received our invite to the Inner City Ministries launch." It was all about making each invitee feel noticed and valued. It worked wonders, turning our event into a gathering everyone was talking about.

Here's how it played out: Delicious food on the table, the one-pager within easy reach, and the palpable energy of a community rallying for a cause.

A Sample Agenda of Your Gathering

Your overall flow to the event can vary, but this is a simple way to look at a timeline. You can adjust the times accordingly. This is planned for two hours:

- 7:00 p.m. — First guests begin to arrive
- 7:15 p.m. — Icebreaker
- 7:30 p.m. — Mingling time (unstructured)
- 7:50 p.m. — Share about your cause or ministry
- 8:15 p.m. — Group photo
- 8:25 p.m. — Mingling time (unstructured)
- 8:45 p.m. — Announce the gathering will end soon
- 9:00 p.m. — Gathering ends. Tell everyone you need your beauty sleep!

How to Navigate the First Twenty Minutes

The first twenty minutes of any event can feel most stressful. Author

Nick Gray calls this window of time the Awkward Zone, and it's something that nearly every gathering goes through. (We highly recommend his handy book, *The 2-Hour Cocktail Party*. Don't worry; you don't have to serve alcohol to gain value from it.)

Anything can happen in these first twenty minutes. Some may show up on time while others trickle in late. Weather or traffic may also cause people to be a bit frazzled on the way to the gathering, and you never know who is going to show up in what order. For those who arrive early or on time, it can feel like everyone is waiting for something to happen so they can stop plodding through the initial forced greetings.

If a guest arrives early or is the first to arrive, tell them you're happy they've arrived and celebrate that they're among the first.

"*Steve! Welcome! Wow, you're the first to arrive. I'm so glad you're here; tonight is going to be a lot of fun.*"

That's it! Don't apologize for the lack of attendees. Enlist the help of your initial guests to help navigate the Awkward Zone. Many guests would rather have something to do than sit on the couch alone, waiting for the party to start. These are some tasks you might ask for help with:

- Coat check
- Writing guests' first names on their beverage cups with a marker
- Serving beverages
- Setting up the snacks or table
- Greeting people at the door with a high-five

All of these tasks give that person a chance to connect with everyone who comes to the gathering in a natural, organic way. Oh, and please have some music playing in the background. No one wants to walk into a gathering that feels like a library!

Icebreakers

After a few people arrive, you can start with an initial round of icebreaker questions. Mike has hosted these kinds of events throughout the years, and he will typically have each person in the room answer these questions:

1. What's your name?
2. What do you do for work?
3. [icebreaker question]

The key here is to use questions that are quick and easy to answer. You don't want to open with questions that force people to be really vulnerable or think too hard, like "What is your greatest fear?" or "What's the best piece of advice you've ever received?"

A simple (and safe) question might be, "What's your favorite breakfast food?" While this might sound too easy, childish, or even irrelevant, the point of the icebreaker is to make each person relatable. Remember, this event is about gathering people together so they can hear about your ministry. You don't want to run the risk of someone going into a ten-minute life story during your icebreaker.

If that question doesn't sit well with you, you can ask questions like these:

- What's the title of the last book you read?
- What's the first job you got paid to do?
- What was your first online screen name, and why?

A few chapters ago, we also talked about the concept of "giving the gift of going second." Take the same approach here and answer your own questions first. This way, you set the example for how people can share their answers.

Once everyone goes, simply transition everyone out of the icebreaker, and you can then reconvene after twenty or so minutes.

"Thanks, everyone! We just did this icebreaker, and there are great people here. Go grab a snack or drink, say hi to someone new, and we'll gather back together in about twenty minutes!"

Now that you've got folks warmed up, they know a little more about each other and find mingling and talking much easier.

When everyone reconvenes, you'll have the opportunity to share about your ministry. This is the time to share your passion, the mission, and the impact your work is having. Let them know how deeply their involvement could resonate and make a difference. Offer clear and inviting steps for how everyone can jump in and be part of this incredible journey.

If you have people from your team at the event, you may ask them ahead of time to share a little about why they decided to join you. Having both new and existing supporters in the same room creates a beautiful sense of community. This is still another reason why it's so important to enlist a team.

What If Someone Declines the Invitation?

If someone you invited decides not to come to your event, try not to take it personally. Their absence can actually be another opportunity in disguise. Someone missing out means you've got a perfect reason to reach out again.

Once your event is done, you'll have pictures and stories to share. You'll be able to bring up the highlights, talk about the new supporters who joined your cause, and really paint a picture of what a special night it was. This opens up two possibilities. First, you can extend an invitation to your next event, giving them another chance to be part of something meaningful. Second, you could suggest catching up one-on-one, making it a more personal invitation to connect. It's all about keeping the conversation going and bridging that gap, inching closer to getting their support for your cause.

Hosting a fundraising event isn't just about gathering people to ask for support; it's about creating a space where the heart of your mission beats loudly and where stories of impact resonate with others. When you take the time to put things like this into motion, great things tend to happen. You'll be known for more than just your work; you'll be known as a connector and someone who brings great people together. Remember, every handshake, every story shared, and every donation received is a step toward a greater impact.

***

Download the workbook we've made available for you at FullyFundedAcademy.com. While you're there, consider enrolling in Fully Funded Academy to get even more training, resources, accountability, and coaching so you can get fully funded, faster.

In Closing

Well, here we are! We've covered a lot of ground, and there's a good amount of work to be done. But we want to remind you that the work will be well worth it. So, here are a few questions for you:

- Are you ready to step up into a bigger vision?
- Are you ready to raise support in a strategic way?
- Are you ready to dramatically grow your current support base?
- Are you ready to step into everything that more financial stability would mean for you?
- Are you ready to provide more resources for the people you serve?
- Are you ready to make a bigger impact on the world?

We hope and pray you answer with a resounding yes!

We're all called to share the Great Commission. More than ever, both of us have a deep appreciation that we are all "part of the body." In the same way the Lord led the two of us together, He led us to the many missionaries we've been able to serve over the years. Now you're here, too. We hope this book has helped you see things in new ways, given you hope, and can serve as a practical and actionable guide for you.

None of us has everything figured out for ourselves, but when we come together and bring the unique experiences and abilities God has given us to the table, amazing things can happen. If you'd like to join us in Fully Funded Academy, along with hundreds of other incredible missionaries and ministry leaders, check out FullyFundedAcademy.com. We'd love to have you.

It's been an absolute honor to serve you. We pray you will be fully funded and have much more than you need for the work you've been called to do.

For His glory,
Mary Valloni and Mike Kim

Acknowledgments

Mary would like to acknowledge the following:

It's difficult to express the full-circle journey this book represents for me. It began with my first fundraising efforts, selling chocolate candy bars for our Christian school fundraiser in elementary school. What seemed so small at such a young age turned into an entrepreneurial journey and a series of promises from the Lord.

In my early twenties, it was clear that I was being called into mission work, where I raised my own personal support. During that time, I knew God was showing me that my work would transcend denominations and geographic boundaries. Over the past decade, I've witnessed God weave together the seeds He planted in my heart as a child into the work I do today.

This book is the product of decades, perhaps generations, with more contributors than I could possibly count, but I'll try my best to acknowledge just a few in my inner circle.

To my family, who inspired and nurtured my curiosity in faith and finances.

To my husband, Geno, and our daughter, Maya, who challenge me to be my best self every day.

To Mike Kim, my partner on this fully funded journey. I am so grateful for your friendship and partnership in this incredible mission we are on.

To all the students who have come through Fully Funded Academy over the years. I am so inspired by each of you. Thank you for letting me be a small part of your journey.

Mike would like to acknowledge the following:

The journey by which this book came to be is one of the most surprising, unexpected, fulfilling, and humbling ones I've ever experienced. The last decade of my life has been a series of redefining seasons. When I stepped away from vocational ministry in 2011, I never thought I'd have direct involvement in it again. My personal life also completely changed during that time, and the things and people who once defined me no longer did.

Yet God's hand has been on my life. I still have a hard time believing this book is done. It's amazing that I've worked with people who are on the frontlines of ministry more than I ever did when on staff at a church. Through this work, I met one of my lifelong friends, Mary Valloni. The Fully Funded community has been my closest community of faith all these years, whether they realize it or not. If you're part of that group and have ever prayed for me, I'm grateful.

God used this work to keep me near Him. I am 100 percent convinced I would not have been able to serve this community or be involved in this project had my life turned out differently.

They say hindsight is 20/20, and I can now see that He took an unconventional guy who lives an unconventional life and had him work with unconventional people who do unconventional things. It's a story only God could write.

Mary Valloni, my dear friend and sister from another mister. I still cannot believe this journey. Words can't express how much you mean to me.

Eric Peoples, God put you in my life so I'd know what a Godly man would look like. I'm honored to be part of your legacy.

Josh Finley, we met as teenagers. Like Kobe and LeBron, we never got to play on the same squad but after all these years I still see you doing your thing in your lane while I'm in mine. Thank you for always cheering me on.

James Harrington, it's amazing we are still in each other's lives. You are one of the most inspiring people I know. I love what you've done with your life.

Robby Fowler, a friend, partner, and brother. Thank you for your support in so many areas of work and life.

Kay Helm, thank you for your help in getting this book started and off the ground! You are a blessing.

My life has been defined by creative pursuits. As diverse as my work has been, there's one verse I've always tucked away as an acknowledgment when I've felt the project has been a God thing: Psalm 109:27. The first was the first album I ever recorded of worship songs I wrote, back when I was in my twenties. The second was my first business book, *You Are the Brand*, in 2021. This is the third.

The verse simply states, "Let them know that it is your hand, that you, LORD, have done it."

About the Authors

Mary Valloni is a respected expert on fundraising, a podcast host, and the award-winning author of the book *Fundraising Freedom*. With over twenty years of fundraising experience with organizations, including the American Cancer Society, the ALS Association, and the Special Olympics, she now shares her expertise as a coach, trainer, and mentor to nonprofit leaders around the world. For more information about Mary, visit MaryValloni.com.

Mike Kim is a marketing strategist and *Wall St. Journal* bestselling author who helps leaders and organizations create impact with their ideas and get their message heard. His clients include faith-based organizations including Catalyst, People of the Second Chance, and Global Mission Awareness, as well as numerous churches, ministry schools, and parachurch organizations. Mike has been featured in and written for *Inc.*, *Entrepreneur*, and *The Huffington Post*. For more information about Mike, visit MikeKim.com.

Grow Your Donor Base, Raise More Support and Get Fully Funded

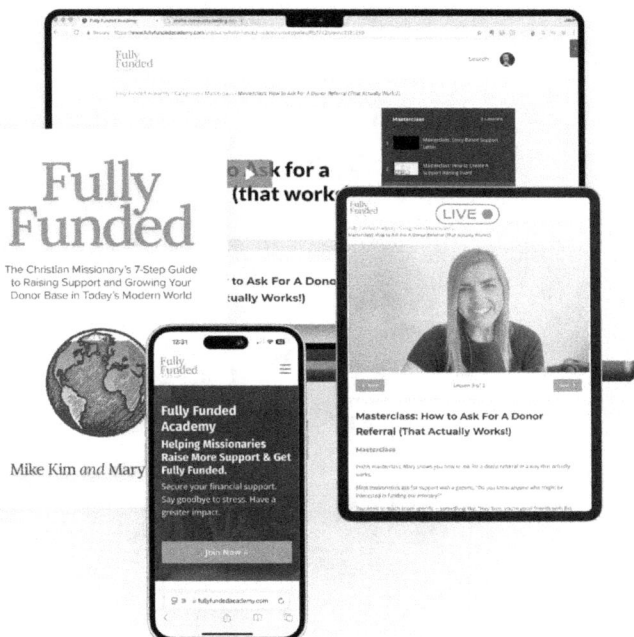

A Proven 7-Part Coaching and Training Program So You Can Communicate with Clarity, Attract More (and Bigger) Donations, and Enjoy Sustainable and Dependable Financial Support.

- Access to the Fully Funded Academy Online Course
- Full Suite of Email and Support Letter Templates
- Bonus In-Depth Masterclasses
- The 7-Step Missionary Support Raising Roadmap

FIND OUT MORE:

fullyfundedacademy.com